guidelines to starting and maintaining a
CHURCH DANCE MINISTRY

Ms. Sonia,
Thank you for your
support + prayers! God Bless!
Denita

guidelines to starting and maintaining a
CHURCH DANCE MINISTRY

Dr. Denita Hedgeman

TATE PUBLISHING & *Enterprises*

Published by Tate Publishing & Enterprises, LLC
127 E. Trade Center Terrace | Mustang, Oklahoma 73064 USA
1.888.361.9473 | www.tatepublishing.com

Tate Publishing is committed to excellence in the publishing industry. The company reflects the philosophy established by the founders, based on Psalms 68:11,
"The Lord gave the word and great was the company of those who published it."

Book design copyright © 2007 by Tate Publishing, LLC. All rights reserved.
Cover design by Jennifer L. Fisher
Interior design by Lindsay B. Behrens

Published in the United States of America

ISBN: 978-1-6024701-9-4
07.07.23

Dedication

To God, my heavenly Father, who solely created me to praise and worship Him through dance. I dedicate my life, body, mind and soul to Him in total holiness. Thank you for the creativity you give me faithfully for every dance to minister, deliver and save souls for your kingdom.

To all of the dance ministries, churches, pastors, bookstores, Bible colleges and seminaries all over the world. May you treasure this book and learn all you can to take your ministries to a higher level in complete anointing and understanding of what God wants in His dance ministry.

To Mississippi Blvd. Christian Church and the Dance Ministry. Thank you so much for allowing me to share the gifts God gave me to cultivate and educate the raw talent of children, youth and adults during classes, Bible study, narrations, worship services, concerts and outreach through the arts. Your support of commitment and example has not only been instrumental in saving and delivering souls but to also aid in the true understanding of the operation of a dance ministry for all who read this book. Dance Ministry, you have now taken the church to the level of divine worship and being free in accepting the spirit through dance!

Table of Contents

Preface

Starting and maintaining an effective dance ministry sounds easy but it takes in depth spiritual knowledge and maturity; physical skill; awareness of other styles, cultures and religions; the ability to recognize the call; and dedicated leadership. Before the research took place for this book, the question had to be asked, "Is Dance Fully Accepted in the Church Today?" Even though the project is about how a dance ministry should run, this question is the underlying element of the whole study. Before a dance ministry can get off the ground, the dance leader needs to know what doctrines other churches and denominations believe; what is the appropriate protocol; the biblical foundation of dance; what God expects of a liturgical dancer; the mandate of the church; the pastor's vision; what types of dances are accepted and not accepted; and how different styles of dance can be incorporated into the worship service.

The objectives of this reference study are to dissect the definitions and differences of secular and liturgical dance; break down the Hebrew and Greek dance terms; understand the original purpose and history of dance; how to start a dance ministry; how to recognize the call; learn the requirements of a dance leader and the members; display guidelines, class format and formations; how to prepare for a worship service, evangelism, a concert and year end annual activities; and learn about liturgical dance organizations.

The information compiled for this study is from the Dictionary; The King James Version of the Holy Bible; The Strongest Strong's Exhaustive Concordance of the Bible; real life experiences through my teaching, ministering, conducting workshops, original writings, guidelines and choreography; surveys on other cultures and denominations; attending International Praise Dance Conferences; feedback from members of the National Liturgical Dance Network and the International Christian Dance Fellowship organizations; and books and manuals from prominent Ministers of Dance and Prophetess' around the world. Other sources are noted in the Bibliography. Also, the Appendix has samples of handouts from workshops I have conducted, dance ministry audition and class guidelines, Bible study questions, concert information, programs, etc.

The information in this study can be used as a general guideline for all dance ministries to follow step by step as they are starting and building their ministry. Also, pastors and church leaders will have the biblical justification to have a dance ministry be an intricate part of the worship service.

1

INTRODUCTION

Is dance fully accepted in the church today? With all of the prejudices, doubts, fears of letting go and being free in the spirit, comparing it to secular dance and the ignorance of not knowing how scripturally based it is, I would still have to say <u>Yes</u>, but not fully. Jeremiah 31:4, 13 refers to Israel's restoration after the war. This relates to the last days when dance will be restored and God's church will be rebuilt:

> Then shall the virgin (bride or church) rejoice in the dance, both young men and old together: for I will turn their mourning into joy, and will comfort them, and make them rejoice from their sorrow[i]. ("Jeremiah 31:13")

In this scripture, maiden/virgin means bride and bride means the church in the last days awaiting for the return of the bridegroom who is Jesus. This is why there are so many dance ministries cropping up in churches now. It was prophesied in the Old Testament and also is the popular thing to do. Unfortunately, some of the pastors, elders, church leaders and ministers of dance do not truly know why they are dancing, what God says about dance in the church, what praise garments (costumes) to wear, what some of the colors mean and how to minister instead of perform for the congregation.

As I travel and conduct dance ministry workshops, the church leaders think that it is something for the youth or girls to do to keep them involved in the church or out of trouble. They do not want to see adults dancing because they think it is disgraceful. They do not know that the Bible wants everyone to dance before the Lord. This means that boys and men can definitely be a part of a dance ministry and dance with all of their might like David did and not worry about it being feminine.

Dance is a part of worship, and everyone is to worship God. When men worship, they run, skip, hop and jump. Most masculine dances focus on warfare, flags, pantomime, ethnical traditions, cultural celebrations or partnering but are not limited to these styles. Before we look at the styles, let us look at the definition of dance.

Definition of Dance

Dance can be defined secularly or spiritually. Dance means secularly to move the body rhythmically to music. To leap and skip about or to bob up and down. A series of rhythmical motions and steps, usually to music.[2] Even though dance is referred to moving to music, there are non—musical, natural movements that people do daily consciously or subconsciously.

Natural Expressions

Some natural movements that people do subconsciously are jumping, running, walking, hand gestures, kicks, dancing around when happy, moving nervously when having to go to the bathroom or stomping when their favorite team is winning during a sports event. Some subconscious movements that people make during a worship service are clapping, shouting, stomping, rocking to music in the congregation/choir and waving arms while praising God or playing the tambourine. Whether naysayers believe it or not, dance is a part of our natural being and the life of the church. We were born to move. Even in a mother's womb, a baby starts to move to his or her mother's waves of breathing, fluids, movements or stillness.

History of Dance/Types

Dance has been around since the beginning of time. People have danced as a part of religious rituals, ceremonies, social celebrations, weddings, births, initiations, baptisms, graduations, birthdays, adulthood, funerals, burials, inaugurations and entertainment. It has been traced through archeological evidence from prehistoric times to the first examples of written and pictorial documentation in 200 BC.[3] The chronological history of dance is outlined below as follows:

A.   1100–*Medieval Times*
(Ballrooms and Court Balls)

B.   1500–*Ethnic Group Movement*
  1.   Ethnic groups from different regions in Africa developed their own individual ceremonial and social dances. It was used to teach, worship, heal and tell stories.

C.   1600–*Church and State Split*
  1.   All arts and guilds started. (If a person was not a guild member, he or she could not dance)
  2.   Court control to kings.
  3.   Minuet dance was invented. (One only touched partner's hand)
  4.   Slaves that had been transported from the West Indies brought dances such as the Banda, Juba, Calenda and Shango to the New World.[4]

D.   1700–*The Age of Enlightenment*
  1.   Court people had a part of all cultural dances.
  2.   Industrial Revolution. (Took men out of field and put them behind machinery)
  3.   The Saturday Night Barn Dance was created. (A big social event)
  4.   Alcohol was accepted into the dancing arena.

5. Slaves on plantations developed the Cake Walk, Snake Hips, Turkey Trot, Truckin and Crop—Over harvest dances.

E. 1790–*The Waltz was Created*
   1. Six thousand people were involved at Apollo Palace in which peasants initiated.
   2. Social class walls were broken down.
   3. Man was put in the role of a partner.

F. 1837–*Seal of Approval Began*

G. 1840–*The Polka was Created*

H. 1850–*The American Frontier*
   1. Square dance was created and saloon dances began.
   2. The Barn Dance. (An out of church event)
   3. Tap dance surfaced when the timbrels were taken from the slaves. (The beat was invented from their shoes)

I. 1860–*Traveling Dance Teachers Surfaced*
   1. Social graces started to influence many individuals.

J. 1900–*Fox Trot Introduced*

K. 1910–*Blacks First Recognition In Off—Broadway Shows*
   1. The Creole Show was the first all black touring off—Broadway show.

L. 1920–*The Charleson Began* (Created by blacks and influenced by the white society)

1. Dance Studies began to be considered a serious academic discipline.
2. Josephine Baker entered the scene in musicals and movies.
3. New York City's Cotton Club became an avenue for black choreographers.

M. 1930–*The Big Band Era* (The Swing was the most popular dance)
1. The New Negro Art Theater Dance Group became the first professional black dance company promoting African and Caribbean dance themes.

N. 1940–*Modern Dance Era For Blacks*
1. Lester Horton started the first integrated modern dance company.

O. 1950–*World War I* (Lost men to war)
1. Latin craze started.
2. Alvin Ailey formed Alvin Ailey American Dance Theater.

P. 1960–*Rock and Roll* ("Sock Hops")
1. Vietnam War
2. Dance Theatre of Harlem was formed.

Q. 1970–*New Wave and Disco Craze*
1. Soul Train featured the most current social dances.

R. 1980–*The Decade of Self Gratification*
1. Exercising and aerobics were popular.
2. Ballet was now in 355 colleges across the nation.
3. The return of dance to the church through the Restoration of David's Tabernacle.

S.   1990–*All Forms of Dance were Accepted*
1.   Dance organizations, companies, etc. around the world were losing national funding and community classes were dropping dance classes first.
2.   Dance and the arts were widely accepted in the church and on a major upswing.

Now in the 2000's, all forms of dance are celebrated, taught and accepted. Some of the other forms not mentioned above are modern, jazz, ethnic, cultural, yoga, line dancing, hip—hop, River Dance, Latin, African, club dancing, etc. Even aerobics, gymnastics, pom pom, Pilates, figure skating, synchronized swimming and martial arts have incorporated movements to music in their presentations.

Liturgical Dance Definition

Liturgical Dance means to dance during public worship in the Christian church. The word "liturgical", comes from the root word "liturgy". Liturgy is defined as an Eucharistic rite. The word Eucharist was what the early church referred to when they spoke of the 'host' or the consecrated bread partaken of during the sacrament of Holy Communion.[5] A rite is ceremonial in nature and is done as a public congregational or community display of celebration. For example, in both the Jewish and African Cultures, traditionally there is a grand observance of the ceremony known as "Rites of Passage". This is where young boys and girls are celebrated as moving from one stage of life to another (Childhood to adulthood). For the Jews, this is formally called a 'bar mitzvah' for males and a 'bat mitzvah' for females. In any case, a rite, when practiced by born again believers, is done specifically as an act of dedication and worship unto God.

Therefore, a liturgical dancer is one who expresses his or her faith through movement ministry in a public worship setting. The goal of this form of expression is to have spiritual communion with God. This is what distinguishes a dancer from the liturgical dancer. The standard is raised in areas such as personal lifestyle, anointing, fellowship with God, prayer, meditation, as well as the content and quality of the dance, which is brought forth before the Father and His people. Even though everyone is a dancer and is called to worship God through praise, thanksgiving and movement, everyone is <u>not</u> called to be a liturgical dancer.

There are many functions and types of liturgical dance in the church and each has its own purpose and style. Depending on one's call, abilities or mantle, a certain style or type of dance might be more natural, effective or suitable for certain situations. Let us look at the purpose of the functions of liturgical dance.

Functions and Significance of Liturgical Dance

The two main functions of liturgical dance are that it tells a story and it gives bodily shape to gratitude or joy. Other functions in the church are: (See Appendix Example #1)

I. *Ministry Unto the Lord*
    As worshippers, it is our first priority to use expressive worship/dance as a way to convey our love to the Lord. Expressive worship is an outward manifestation of an inward emotion that cannot be expressed through words alone. This can be done through a number of dancers, solo dancers, choreographed, spontaneous or prophetic dances. Romans 12:1 tells us that we are to present our bodies (entire being) as a living sacrifice, holy and acceptable of God. This is our reasonable service of worship. It is not enough to justify with our mouths what the heart is feeling. We must show it with our whole being.

II. *Ushering in the Presence of the Lord*
    Dancers should work closely with the singers and musicians. They work corporately to prepare the atmosphere and invite in the Lord's presence.

In 1 Chronicles 15:16, King David uses singing, dancing, musical instruments, processionals and banners to usher in the presence of the Lord:

> And David spake to the chief of the Levites to appoint their brethren to be the singers with instruments of musick, psalteries and harps and cymbals sounding, by lifting up the voice with joy.[6] ("1 Chronicles 15:16")

III. *To Perform Spiritual Warfare*

The word connects dance and warfare many times throughout the Bible. Warfare is defeating the enemy through prayer, praise and dance. The enemy flees when we praise God. We can use our mouths, arms, legs and weapons of war (flags, tambourines, banners) in praise to defeat the enemy. In 2 Chronicles 20:21–22, King Jehoshaphat sent out the singers and "those who should praise" the beauty of His holiness in to battle first. When they obeyed the Lord and praised Him, their enemies were defeated:

> And when he had consulted with the people, he appointed singers unto the Lord, and that should praise the beauty of holiness, as they went out before the army, and to say, Praise the Lord; for his mercy endureth for ever. And when they began to sing and to praise, the Lord set ambushments against the children of Ammon, Moab, and Mount Seir, which were come against Judah; and they were smitten.[7] ("2 Chronicles 20:21–22")

IV. *To Help Lead the People Into His Presence*

Since dancers/singers are worship leaders, they are to help bring people in His presence. Many times, this is accomplished because of the warfare that they have done. Dancers/worshippers are not there for people to spectate or to be entertained; they are there to lead people into participating into worship. Sometimes when people see the worshippers raise their hands, they will do the same. Psalms 150 is a perfect example of corporate praise where after the dancers/singers/worshippers have led the worship service into praise, the whole congregation in the sanctuary can be on one accord:

> Praise ye the Lord. Praise God in his sanctuary: praise him in the firmament of his power. Praise him for his mighty acts: praise him according to his excellent greatness. Praise him with the sound of the trumpet: praise him with the psaltery and harp. Praise him with the timbrel and dance: praise him with stringed instruments and organs. Praise him upon the loud cymbals: praise him upon the high sounding cymbals. Let every thing that hath breath praise the Lord. Praise ye the Lord.[8] ("Psalms 150:1–6")

V. *Intercessory Prayer*

Sometimes dance can be used as a prayer of faith, supplication or deliverance. When people are ushered into the presence of God, they are no longer spectating. Usually worship, repentance, forgiveness and change come as the dancers pray to God through their dance. Colossians 1:9–12 is an example what intercessors or dancers can use when praying for someone to have fully the mind of Christ:

> For this cause we also, since the day we heard it, do not cease to pray for you, and to desire that ye might be filled with the knowledge of his will in all wisdom and spiritual understanding; That ye might walk worthy of the Lord unto all pleasing, being fruitful in every good work, and increasing in the knowledge of God; Strengthened with all might, according to His glorious power unto all patience and long suffering with joyfulness; Giving thanks unto the Father, which hath made

us meet to be partakers of the inheritance of the saints in light.[9] ("Colossians 1:9–12")

VI. *Dance Adds the Important Visual Aspect to Worship*
Seeing is a reality of faith. Hearing plants the seed of faith, but seeing causes fruition. When we can visualize the nature and character of God, we can better understand Him and better worship Him. That is why churches use big productions such as the Passion Play, Christmas productions, New Year's Eve Services, etc. as a witnessing tool. The congregation can actually see the scriptures come to life.

VII. *Dance in the Church is the Fulfillment to Prophecy*

As stated before, Jeremiah 31:4 says that the virgin shall rejoice in the dance in the latter days when we shall see God rebuilding His church. Rejoice and joy in Hebrew is giyl/gil, which means to dance and spin about with strong emotion.[10]

VIII. *Dance is a Sign of Blessings and Restoration in the Church*
2 Samuel 6:13–14 shows the restoration of the Glory of God to His people associated with dance. In this passage, King David brought the Ark of the Covenant from the house of Obededom into the City of David. He praised God with all manner of instruments and dances with all of his might in a linen ephod. God blessed his house and restored the church. Also, in Lamentations 5:15 and Isaiah 16:10a, God shows us that the absence of dance is sign of judgment:

The joy of our heart is ceased; our dance is turned into mourning.[11] ("Lamentations 5:15")

And gladness is taken away, and joy (gil) out of the plentiful field; and in the vineyards there shall be no singing, neither shall there be shouting:[12] ("Isaiah 16:10a")

IX. *Dance is a Sign of the End Times*
There were three main events always associated with dancing in Israel:

Harvest—The End of the World/Feast of the Tabernacles (Feast of His Coming):

> The enemy that sowed them is the devil; the harvest is the end of the world; and the reapers are the angels.[13] ("Matthew 13:39")

Marriage—Marriage of the Lamb (Second Coming of Christ/Jesus for his bride/church):

> Let us be glad and rejoice, and give honour to him: for the marriage of the Lamb is come, and his wife hath made herself ready. And to her was granted that she should be arrayed in fine linen, clean and white: for the fine linen is the righteousness of saints.[14] ("Revelation 19:7–8")

Victories in Battle—The dance of Mahanaim (two armies) A type of Armegeddon or final battle.

> Behold, I come as a thief. Blessed is he that watcheth, and keepeth his garments, lest he walk naked, and they see his shame. And he gathered them together into a place called in the Hebrew tongue Armageddon.[15] ("Revelation 16:15–16")

X. *Dance Can Reach Across Cultural and Politiacl Barriers With the Gospel*
Dance is a non—verbal form of communication and can reach many cultures and languages. Many nations do not allow the preaching of the gospel in more standard forms

(missionaries, Bibles, etc.) but do admit dance and drama groups to minister. It is even better if you know about the other cultures and what their dances and movements mean. It would have more of an impact on them and souls would be saved. In Matthew 28:19–20, Jesus tells us to go into the nations to minister. These instructions are not in a box. It could mean preach, teach, dance, sing, pass out Bibles, prepare dramatizations, etc.:

> Go ye therefore, and teach all nations, baptizing them in the name of the Father, and of the Son, and of The Holy Ghost: Teaching them to observe all things whatsoever I have commanded you: and, lo, I am with you always, even unto the end of the world.[16] ("Matthew 28:19–20")

XI. *Dancing Heralds a New Move in God*
Dance says, "Watch out! Something special is happening here!" In scripture, whenever dance is especially noted, it is in association with significant *New* moves of God.

A. In Exodus 15:20, Miriam led the Israelites into song and dance after The Red Sea experience. This was the first time dance was mentioned in the Bible.

B. In Judges 21, the tribe Jabesh—Gilead did not assemble before the Lord. So the Lord told one of the Israelite tribes, Benjamin, to smite them; even the women and children. The Lord spared 400 virgins and let the men of the tribe of Benjamin take them as wives. Since it was not enough of virgins for them, the elder of the congregation told them to go to hide in the vineyards of Shiloh and wait until the daughters of Shiloh came out to dance. When the daughters came out, they took them as wives. After they explained their situation to the daughters' fathers and brothers, they released them to go with the tribe of Benjamin.

Natural Expressions of Liturgical Dance in Church

Some natural expressions that worshippers do in the church during worship service are:

Standing—It is an international sign of respect toward someone. It shows attentiveness. When someone of royalty comes into a room, it is protocol to stand in honor and respect towards that person. We are encouraged in scripture to stand and worship the Lord who is King of Kings. The Bible states:

> Ye that stand in the house of the Lord, in the courts of the house of our God.[17] ("Psalms 135:2")

Kneeling—We kneel as an act of reverence and submission in awe of something sacred.

> O come, let us worship and bow down: let us kneel before the Lord our maker.[18] ("Psalms 95:6")

Bowing Down—To bend the head or body in respect or recognition. To yield or submit to authority. Three Hebrew words for bowing during worship are *Shachah* which is used 171 times, *Qudad* which is used 15 times and *Kara* which is used 30 times. The Greek word for bowing is *Proskuneo*, which means to be prostrate before God or to kiss towards.

> I have sworn by myself, the word is gone out of my mouth in righteousness, and shall not return, That unto me every knee shall bow, every tongue shall swear.[19] ("Isaiah 45:23")

The Lifting of Hands—There are 12 different reasons given in the scriptures for the lifting of hands:

1.   In Supplication—Earnest request for help.

>   Hear the voice of my supplications, when I cry unto thee, when I lift up my hands toward thy holy oracle.[20] ("Psalms 28:2")

2.   Repentance—Cleanse your heart before God. Feeling remorse for wrongdoing.

>   Let us search and try our ways, and turn again to the Lord. Let us lift up our heart with our hands unto God in the heavens.[21] ("Lamentations 3:40–41")

3.   General Prayer Habit—Always seen in the church during corporate praise.

>   Let my prayer be set forth before thee as incense; and the lifting up of my hands as the evening sacrifice.[22] ("Psalms 141:2")

4.   To Bless and Praise God—It is the ultimate will to praise God as stated in 1 Thessalonians 5:16–23. We were created to praise and bless the Lord that is also stated in Psalms 63:4.

>   Thus will I bless thee while I live: I will lift up my hands in thy name.[23] ("Psalms 63:4")

5.   Worship—An act of reverence and adoration of who God is and not for what He has done.

>   If we have forgotten the name of our God, or stretched out our hands to a strange god; Shall not God search this out? for he knoweth the secrets of the heart.[24] ("Psalms 44:20")

6.   Thirsting and Seeking after God—Having a genuine hunger for God.

I stretch forth my hands unto thee: my soul thirsteth after thee, as a thirsty land. Se'lah.[25] ("Psalms 143:6")

7.   War/Warfare— Coming against the enemy so hard with praise and worship that he has to leave.

And it came to pass, when Moses held up his hand, that Israel prevailed: and when he let down his hand, Amalek prevailed. But Moses hands were heavy; and they took a stone, and put it under him, and he sat thereon; and Aaron and Hur stayed up his hands, the one on the one side, and the other on the other side; and his hands were steady until the going down of the sun.[26] ("Exodus 17:11–12")

8.   Seeking Divine Power from God—Looking for a sign of power. In Exodus, Moses stretched out his hands with his rod showing God's power:

But lift thou up thy rod, and stretch out thine hand over the sea, and divide it: and the children of Israel shall go on dry ground through the midst of the sea.[27] ("Exodus 14:16")

9.   Meditation of the Word—As we sing or pray, we should think and meditate on the Word of God.

My hands also will I lift up unto thy commandments, which I have loved; and I will meditate in thy statutes.[28] ("Psalms 119:48")

10.   To Bless Others—We were created to praise and worship God and to bless others. When praises go up, blessings come down. So when blessings come down, they come down on everyone around at the same place.

> And he (Jesus) led them out as far as to Bethany, and he lifted up his hands, and blessed them.[29] ("Luke 24:50")

11. When We Make a Solemn Oath or Declaration—In the court system, people under oath put their hand on the Bible and raise their right hand up and swear to tell the truth. When we lift up our hands, it is sign to the heavens that our life stands behind whatever statement we are proclaiming:

> And I heard the man clothed in linen, which was upon the waters of the river, when he held up his right hand and his left hand unto heaven, and sware by him that liveth for ever that it shall be for a time, times, and an half; and when he shall have accomplished to scatter the power of the holy people, all these things shall be finished.[30] ("Daniel 12:7")

12. The Sign as the State of the Heart—The outward is a sign of what is happening inwardly. If one is happy on the inside, then it will show through their dancing. The movements will beam through them. The same goes to if a dancer is tired or sad, then their movements will appear weak.

> Wherefore lift up the hands which hang down, and the feeble knees;[31] ("Hebrews 12:12")

Clapping of the Hands—To strike the hands together to produce a sharp percussive noise. There are six ways that clapping of the hands was used in the Bible:

1. Rejoicing—Feeling joy or great delight.

> For ye shall go out with joy, and be led forth with peace: the mountains and the hills shall break forth

before you into singing, and all the trees of the field shall clap their hands.[32] ("Isaiah 55:12")

2.   In the Coronation of a King—When someone was proclaimed King everyone would clap their hands during the crowning of him.

> And he brought forth the king's son, and put the crown upon him, and gave him the testimony; and they made him king, and anointed him; and they clapped their hands, and said, God save the king.[33] ("2 Kings 11:12")

3.   In Triumph of God—Used as a release for the people.

> O Clap your hands, all ye people; shout unto God with the voice of triumph.[34] ("Psalms 47:1")

4.   Anger—An Old Testament tradition or when God showed his vengeance against people who sinned against Him. In the scripture below, God was angry with the Israelites and was going to destroy them for being wicked.

> I will also smite mine hands together, and I will cause my fury to rest: I the Lord have said it.[35] ("Ezekiel 21:17")

5.   Contempt—The feelings or actions toward something/someone considered worthless, low, beneath. Lack of respect or reverence for something. In Biblical times, people clapped toward the enemy when they were about to go to war. In modern times, we are to hiss and clap at the devil, drive him out or scoff him away.

> Men shall clap their hands at him (Satan), and shall hiss him out of his place.[36] ("Job 27:23")

6.   Sorrow—Deep distress and regret.

Thus saith the Lord God; Smite with thine hand, and stamp with thy foot, and say, Alas for all the evil abominations of the house of Israel! for they shall fall by the sword, by the famine, and by the pestilence.[37] ("Ezekiel 6:11")

Types of Liturgical Dance

There are different types of dance in the church. Most are done according to the flow of the service or what vision the pastor has for a sermon. Sometimes the Holy Spirit has a global message that he is conveying for a couple of Sundays in a series form or that other pastors from other churches are teaching. The whole church might be going through financial difficulty or abuse. The dance ministry leader should be sensitive to those needs and choreograph certain dances that deal with those issues. The dances should never be entertaining; they should always minister to the needs. Some churches and pastors have to be educated to be open to allow the dance ministry to minister the way that God is leading. Some churches that are not operating in all of the gifts of the Holy Spirit or prophetically will plan for the dance ministry to <u>perform</u> during the service to fill in dead spots or to entertain the congregation. They are aware that dance ministries are booming all across the country, so they want to make sure that they have one also.

In Romans 12, Paul states that we have many members in one body, but all the members do not have the same office. They all complement each other for the total operation of the body. One member cannot function without the other. The same is in dancing in the church. There are different types for different situations, sermons, seasons, celebrations, ceremonies or events. Let us look at some of them. (See Appendix Example #2)

Praise Dance—This is a choreographed, pre—rehearsed dance that displays the joy and celebration of what God has done for us. It is usually upbeat and sometimes repetitive. In most churches, it is done live with the praise singers and minister of music. Some churches will have a pre—recorded song, but it still ushers in the presence of the Lord and the congregation into worship.

In 1 Thessalonians 5:16–18, it tells us to rejoice evermore, pray without ceasing and in everything give thanks unto God. It lets us know that this is the will of God concerning us. In Psalms 146:1–2, tells us to praise the Lord while we are living and have any being.

Dance is mentioned for the first time in the Bible in Exodus. It shows that the Israelites are in praise after they crossed the Red Sea and Pharaoh and his men were drowned during their quest to recapture them, even though he told Israelites they could leave Egypt. They had been in slavery in Egypt for years. Miriam, the prophetess, led them in a prophetic/praise dance and song:

> For the horse of Pharaoh went in with his chariots and with his horsemen into the sea, and the Lord brought again the waters of the sea upon them; but the children of Israel went on dry land in the midst of the sea. And Miriam the prophetess, the sister of Aaron, took a timbrel in her hand; and all the women went out after her with timbrels and with dances. And Miriam answered them, Sing ye to the Lord, for he hath triumphed gloriously; the horse and his rider hath he thrown into the sea.[38] (Exodus 15:19–21)

Once the congregation is up and praising, the dance ministry can lead them into congregational dance.

Congregational Dance—Congregational dancing is when the praise dancers are leading the congregation into easy praise dance steps. The steps are repetitive and everyone is on one accord with the singers and musicians. God says to praise him in the congregation of saints in the dance, singing and with all manner of instruments.

> Praise ye the Lord. Sing unto the Lord a new song, and his praise in the congregation of saints. Let Israel rejoice in him that made him: let the children of Zion be joyful in their King. Let them praise his name in the dance: let

them sing praises unto him with the timbrel and harp. For the Lord taketh pleasure in his people: he will beautify the meek with salvation. Let the saints be joyful in glory: let them sing aloud upon their beds. Let the high praises of God be in their mouth, and a two—edged sword in their hand; To execute vengeance upon the heathen, and punishments upon the people; To bind their kings with chains, and their nobles with fetters of iron; To execute upon them the judgment written: this honour have all his saints. Praise ye the Lord. [39] ("Psalms 149:1–9")

There is power in numbers. Matthew 18:20 states that God is in the midst of two or three gathered in his name. When everyone is on one accord praising God, the presence of the Lord is ushered in and worship is taking place. The enemy has fled because he can not stand to be in the presence of praise. This moves us into the next phase of the service and another type of dance.

Worship Dance—As we praise God, the Holy Spirit brings us into worship. It cannot just be turned on; it is a response to our praise. Praise is thanking God for what He has done and worship is loving Him for who He is. Our one—on—one relationship will show this during this phase of the service. Worship could last for hours because the Holy Spirit is in control. It is during worship that God may decide to speak to us through spoken word, a prophetic dance, a prophetic song or a prophetic drama. This is when people might get healed, encouraged, exhorted, directed, corrected or shown what the mind of Christ is for the hour. [40] Usually worship music is slow and the movements are ballet type. Some people might bow down, cry, speak in their prayer language (tongues), run, walk, sing, punch out the devil warfare steps, laugh, etc.

Prophetic Dance—This dance is initiated by the Holy Spirit during worship. It is spontaneous steps inspired by the Holy Spirit. He might choose a single person out of the group, the leader, the entire group, the pastor or someone from the congregation. God usually has a specific message that He wants danced before the congregation. Sometimes, the singers might sing the words or a prophecy, and the dancers will dance to it. These songs and dances are not rehearsed, but everyone is on one accord. The prophetic dance can be done accapella; to a drum beat, in silence; done to the rhythm of clapping hands, stomping feet, snapping fingers; a dance of warfare; a dance of instruction; a dance of edification; or a dance foretelling the world of events that are about to take place.

An example of a prophetic dance in the Bible was in 1 Samuel 18. After David killed Goliath, the women of Israel came out singing, dancing and prophesying that he had killed 10,000 men when at that point he had only killed a lion, a bear and Goliath.

God works in order. He is going to use a person or people who already know how to work in the prophetic outside of dance ministry. When the Holy Spirit calls someone to do something, He equips them to do it. That is why we are instructed to "study to show ourselves approved." We are representing Him and we cannot dishonor His name. This type of dance will be more effective when the musicians, the worship leader, the dance leader and the pastor learn to flow together.

In 1 Samuel 19:18–24, Elisha and Samuel had a school of the prophets that trained them how to operate in the prophetic. Today, some churches have prophetic conferences that teach people how to use their gifts and allow them to practice, give direction, show correction and whatever else is necessary. Also, 1 Samuel 10:5–6 talks about when Samuel anointed Saul and sent him to the garrison hill of the Philistines. He was greeted by a company of prophets that came down from the high place with a tabret, psaltery, pipe and harp. They prophesied over him. This moved Saul to prophesy. When the Glory of the Lord fills a place the whole congregation might prophesy.

Warfare Dance—This dance is used as well as praise dance to prepare the atmosphere for the preaching of the Word. Sometimes before the worship services starts, there might be a spirit of oppression, depression, sexual sin, jealousy, discord or financial debt lurking around in the sanctuary. It is, usually, hard to dance at first because the atmosphere is heavy. Once the praise, worship, prophetic and warfare dances start, the heaviness is lifted and those spirits leave.

Warfare dance is an aggressive dance filled with sharp movements and sounds such as kicks, stabbing motions, falling, struggle—type moves, punches, feet stomping, death blows, loud cymbals, drums, marching, yelling and praying out loud in tongues or in English. It can include marching around the sanctuary, a block or community; carrying of flags and banners; starting out with the praise and worship dance team and ending up with the whole congregation involved. It could, also, start out with anger at what the devil has stolen from us and end up with shouts of victory as a breakthrough is sensed in the spirit realm.

Usually, women have a natural gift of plunging themselves into worship, but men have a natural gift of warfare. Men and women can do either, but a godly man has the ability to bring forth a double blow to the kingdom of darkness by accepting and maintaining his role as king, priest, and warrior. He has been given the authority to call forth 'Death' to that which has been struck by the woman.[41] That is why David was always a man after God's own heart. He was a praiser, worshipper and warrior that danced before God with all of his might.

There is power in the feet. Our feet serve as shock absorbers for the entire body and have the largest and strongest tendon in the human body—the Achilles Tendon. This tendon connects the calf muscles to the heel of the foot. This is why God's promise of Satan's impending doom is so powerful when we strike his heel. We utilize the power of the heel to destroy him and cut him down! He, then, comes under our authority through Jesus Christ, who has proclaimed that He Himself has placed all things 'under His feet'.

And the God of peace shall bruise Satan under your feet shortly. The grace of our Lord Jesus Christ be with you. Amen.[42] ("Romans 16:20")

Dance of Travail—The dance of travail is a dance of faith where we thank God for the answer to our prayer before the answer is visible. It is similar to war dance. One can travail through prayer by speaking the Word and praying in the spirit. The Holy Spirit may give movements of warfare, supplication, expressing power and authority or a combination of several things. The movements are usually circular or crouching as in giving birth. It is more of a victory dance because by faith you already know what the outcome of the situation you are dancing even though the manifestation is not evident at that time. A dance team can give a prophecy or rhema word for the church, pastor, elders or a person in the congregation:

> Who hath heard such a thing? Who hath seen such things? Shall the earth be made to bring forth in one day? Or shall a nation be born at once? For as soon as Zion travailed, she brought forth her children.[43] ("Isaiah 66:8")

Dance of Celebration/Festival—To celebrate means to commemorate, engage in festivities, ceremonialize, exalt or cheer. A dance can celebrate the birth of Jesus Christ, the resurrection of Jesus Christ the soon coming Bridegroom (Christ), a personal, corporate or family victory or any event of the liturgical calendar.

In the Old Testament, the Israelites were commanded by God to appear before Him in the sanctuary three times a year. They were commanded to celebrate the Passover in Deuteronomy 16:1; the Feast of Harvest, which in the New Testament is known as the Day of Pentecost when the Holy Spirit fell on the disciples in the upper room in Acts 2:1–4 and in the Old Testament in Exodus 23:16; and the Feast of Tabernacles mentioned in Deuteronomy 16:13–15. This was a feast to celebrate the harvest.

The three festivals that were prevalent in the New Testament while Jesus was on earth were the Feast of Passover in the Gospel of

Matthew, Feast of Tabernacles and The Day of Pentecost. During the Feast of Passover, Jesus cleansed the temple by saying that the temple should be a house of prayer. As dancers, we should be people of prayer and not contaminate our bodies with things of the world. This feast was also associated with healing. Exodus 12 and Psalms 105:37 tell us that Israel was healed as they fed upon the body of the Passover Lamb. It is also associated with the body and the blood of Jesus. Jesus did the miracle of the feeding of the multitude and taught His disciples that He was the bread of life during the Feast of Passover. As dancers, we should always be prayed up and filled with the Holy Spirit so that we can be used as channels to bring healing to the congregation.

The second was the Feast of Tabernacles, which was marked by peculiar rites, sacrifices, joyous festivities and dwelling in booths. In this account Jesus triumphantly entered Jerusalem with the people waving palm branches as He passed them. This feast also included a ceremony of the drawing out of waters. This spoke of the Holy Spirit who would be poured out when Jesus was glorified. The processional dances that are associated with this festival today are the torch dance, marching, and people and children singing while carrying flags and candles.

The last festival was the Day of Pentecost. This festival was not only a symbol of the outpouring of the Holy Spirit, but also the uniting of the Jews and Gentiles into one body. During this feast, the people rejoiced as they thanked God for the plentiful harvest, and they offered it unto the Lord. As they marched to the appointed place of gathering, the people rejoiced as they marched to the music. A dance of celebration can be done in a circle, solo, group, in a spontaneous fashion or in a choreographic form. The movements will usually express joy, honor, exaltation, cheer and reverence. These movements can be leaping, skipping, jumping, twirling, walking, hand clapping or with tambourines.

Processionals—In the Bible, most of the dances and celebrations were done as a processional. The most appropriate part of the service is to march in with flags, candles, singers, deacons, elders or the pastor at the beginning of the service. Most of the movements are walking, marching, running, skipping, turning, clapping stomping, etc. These steps are usually done in coming down the aisles. Psalms 68:24–25 shows that it is appropriate for singers and dancers to process down the aisles. (See Appendix Example #3)

> They have seen thy goings, O God; even the goings of my God, my King, in the sanctuary. The singers went before, the players on instruments followed after; among them were the damsels playing with timbrels.[44] ("Psalms 68:24–25")

Ceremonial Dancing—There are times when a liturgical dancer or dance team may be asked to minister at some of the following ceremonies or services:

1. Ordinations—They can be choreographed specifically to those being ordained or with a theme to the congregation. A processional can be prepared before the service to show the solemnity and holiness of the occasion.

2. Weddings—These dances can be choreographed to beautiful songs about the bride and groom to show the covenant between a husband and wife. There can also be a round dance celebrating the union.

3. Funerals—These dances can show the union of the departed soul with God in Heaven if the family of the departed is in agreement to have this done. God may choose to manifest Himself through a prophetic dance.

4. Baby Dedications—These dances can celebrate the new life or to speak goodness into the life of the child and family.

5. Birthdays—These dances can celebrate another year of the person's life or prophetically show what God has in store for him or her in the future.

6. Rites of Passage—These dances celebrate when a boy makes the transition from a child to a man. They are ritualistic and are of the Jewish culture.

7. Graduations—These dances are dignified and formal. Processions are usually the most effective. If they are choreographed, they focus on the celebration of one's embarking on a new season of their life.

8. Evangelistic Services—These can be a concert sponsored by the church for the purpose of evangelism. They can be held at church, a community center, a park, a theater, a nursing home or on the beach. They could have a variety of styles to appeal to all types of people.

Tambourine Dancing—Tambourines were used in warfare, Jewish dances and to celebrate victory. They were also used in Praise and Worship. In Exodus 15, Miriam was the first person that was mentioned in the Bible who danced. Her prophetic dance was a victory dance to celebrate the Israelites crossing the Red Sea. Other dance accounts in the Bible were when David triumphantly defeated Goliath in battle or when he brought the Ark of Covenant to the City of David. Tambourines were used during these victories.

God loves music and instruments. He commands in Psalms 149 and 150 to praise Him with all types of instruments including timbrels (tambourines). ("Jeremiah 31:4") mentions tabrets, which also means tambourines.

Flags/Banners/Billow Banners—Flags wave God's blessings unto the congregation. They are the covering of the Lord. Dancers can sit, pray, dance or run under it. This signifies that they are under the presence of the Lord.

> Deep calleth unto deep at the noise of thy waterspouts: all thy waves and thy billows are gone over me.[45] ("Psalms 42:7")

They, also, represent in the Bible a tribe or family, ("Numbers 2:2; 10:10–14") Warfare, ("Psalms 20:5; 74:4"; "Isaiah 31:9") a rallying point, ("Isaiah 5:26; 11:10") and as a proclamation ("Jeremiah 4:6; 51:12"; "Isaiah 62:10"; "Psalms 60:4").

Streamers/Ribbons—Streamers and ribbons also wave God's blessings over the congregation. Certain movements have biblical meanings. Moving them in a circular motion over your head to the right means "Hallelujah;" moving them in a circular motion over your head to the left means "Reverse Hallelujah;" moving them in a circular motion in front of your body clockwise means "Alpha;" moving them in a circular motion in front of your body counter clockwise means "Omega;" moving them in a figure eight means "Faithfulness;" moving them in two half circles in front of the body means "Banner Over Me;" and moving them squiggly from left to right in front of the body means "Gloria."

Interpretive Dancing—This dance interprets the words to a song, scripture or Bible story. It is very detailed and usually done to slow music. The movements can be ballet, smooth and of reverence. Before the church, leaders, pastors and dance teams really knew what liturgical dance was, they just called the dance of the church interpretive or just liturgical thinking they meant ballet movements. They did not know that liturgical means dances of the church according to the liturgy calendar. In some cases, interpretive dances can be done in a fast manner. This kind of dance brings the Word to light.

Drama—This is similar to interpretive dance. Usually, actors and actresses act out Biblical stories with skits, plays and dances. Most churches love to dramatize the Calvary, Resurrection and the birth of Christ. They make it a big celebration with costumes and props.

Choreo—drama—This is a story mixed with acting and dancing. It is very effective when the scenarios can relate to real life issues such as drugs, suicide, debt, gang violence or other sins. The acting is done in a pulsated rhythm to the words and music while dancing. Some churches call it a human video.

Pantomime—This is a great evangelistical dance because Christians and non—Christians can relate to it and not be offended. It is light and sometimes comical. It is similar to a choreo—drama in that dancing and acting are choreographed together while doing illusional movements. Usually, the faces are painted white, and the movements go with every word of the song. Advanced pantomimes can look like they are sitting in a chair, leaning against an imaginary wall, enclosed in a box, walking or running in place.

Types of Liturgical Groups

As dance ministries are growing rapidly all over the world, they are categorizing themselves by certain groups and names according to their purpose, church vision, denomination, region, country or creative strength. If some groups are limited in dance technique, they might focus on arm movements, acting, sign language or something easier. The following types of groups fit into this category:

Praise Dancers—They usually minister during praise and worship displaying repetitive movements with the congregation, minister of music and the singing praise team. Sometimes the dances are not choreographed. A leader stands in front of the other dancers and come up with the steps while the other dancers follow. The congregation is also following along with the steps.

Worship Dancers—The dancers lead the congregation into worship. They are usually prophetic and are able to interpret what the Holy Spirit is conveying to the congregation through dance. Their movements are reverent and smooth. They might do a lot of bowing and kneeling. The movements are very simple and not intimidating.

Sacred Dancers—It is the same as a liturgical dancer. It is the dance of the church during a public worship service. Sacred emphasizes the holiness of the ministry and the intimate relationship that the dancer has with God. Sacred means to be set apart. The dances focus on God's holiness and the respect of Him.

Dance Choirs—This is popular in the East. Dancers are set—up in the choir stand in about 4–6 rows like a choir, but they do easy arm movements, sways and other movements to praise music.

Dance Chorales—A small group of dancers and singers that ministers to organ music, hymns or sacred music.

Davidic Dancers—Dancers that emphasize the Jewish culture, warfare dances of David, the Star of David and the Lion of Judah. The movements are upbeat, springy and festive.

Dance Dramatists—It is similar to drama, choreo—drama and pantomime. They act out Biblical scenes through dance.

Dance Team—Most churches call their dance ministry a dance team not realizing that is secularizing the name. They do not understand or conceive how dancers are to minister. They want a good performance during worship service. In the school system, the dancers are called a dance team. For church it should be different. It should be set apart.

With all of these names, types and titles of dance groups and teams, it is still deeper and more of a calling when one is called to be a liturgical dancer. God holds them to a deeper ministry accountability and intimate relationship with Him. It is not about performing, but about ministering to the people about Jesus Christ. A dance should be just as effective as a sermon. It should save souls and encourage the saints.

> Whether therefore ye eat, or drink, or whatsoever ye do,
> do all to the glory of God.[46] ("1 Corinthians 10:31").

The Liturgical/Christian Calendar

During the regular calendar certain holidays are celebrated and people go all the way out during the commemoration period. Schools, churches and jobs close; stores sell decorations and offer discounts; people give parties and travel and television shows showcase celebratory specials. These secular holidays give honor to a certain group of people for what they have done.

The Christian calendar sets up a cycle of corporately remembering what Christ has done for us. Liturgical dancers should always have dances prepared according to the Christian calendar. Most churches celebrate the church year which commemorates the sufferings of Jesus, His life, death, resurrection, ascension and second coming. Let us look at the events during the church year.

Advent—The calendar begins here. Advent means "coming" or "arrival." It represents the time preceding the birth of Christ. In the sixth century, it was the six weeks before Christmas.[47] The purpose of this celebration is to prepare the people for the coming of Christ as a babe in Bethlehem and for his second coming.

Christmas—This season consists of twelve days and ends with Epiphany. The twelve days are between December 25 and January 6. The liturgies of this period are centered around Matthew and Luke's Biblical accounts of the baby Jesus.

Epiphany—It means manifestation in Greek. It refers to the baptism of Jesus at which God revealed that Jesus was His beloved Son, and He was pleased with Him. This is stated in Mark 1:9–11. Today, it is celebrated on the closest Sunday to January 6.

Lent—Lent, which in Latin means "springtime," is a six—week period of spiritual discipline before Resurrection Sunday. It begins with Ash Wednesday. It has now come to mean the preparation for the death of Christ as well as the death of our own sins in Christ. This is a time when Christians take a close look at their lives and examine their spiritual walk with the Lord. They ask God to show them things in their lives that they need to repent.

Holy Week—This is centered around the Great Triduum, the three days from Thursday through Saturday evening when Jesus was crucified and the night before he was raised from the dead.

Maundy Thursday—This commemorates the events of the night Jesus was arrested. It is associated with the last meal he had with his disciples and when he gave the commandment "To love one another" (John 13:34). It is, also, a symbol of the ceremonial washing of the feet of the poor.

Good Friday—This was from noon to 3:00 P.M. when Jesus hung on the cross.

Holy Saturday—This was a day of prayer, fasting, meditation and fasting in preparation for the great paschal vigil. This is the most important service because it is a celebration of the death and resurrection of Christ. This service is either at 11:00 p.m. or 5:00 a.m. The paschal candle is lit signifying the resurrection life of Christ bursting from the grave. Scripture is read, baptism is given to those who are prepared and the Lord's Supper is celebrated.

Easter—This is the celebration of the Christ's resurrection from the grave. In the ancient church, the Easter season lasted fifty days. The preaching during this time was centered around the post—resurrection appearances of Jesus, his re—appearance to his disciples and the disciples' preparation to declare the kingdom of God. It ended on Pentecost Sunday.

Pentecost Sunday—This was the celebration of the coming of the Spirit of the Lord.

Hebrew and Greek Dance Terms

Dance is in the Bible several times in English, Hebrew or Greek. The English vocabulary is limited because it only refers specifically to dance in the Old and New Testament about 27 times using the words dance, danced, dances and dancing. Other English words referring to dance in the Bible are praise, worship, bow, jump, skip, turn, leap, etc.

Since the Old Testament was translated from Hebrew and the New Testament was translated from Greek, there are 16 Hebrews words that related to dance in the Old Testament and 8 Greek words that related to dance in the New Testament. In the Old Testament, dance was mentioned when it related to worship, celebrations, victory, warfare, festivals and restoration. In the New Testament, it was related to celebrations, evil, (seductive) healing or faith. The words below are referenced from the Strongest Strong's Exhaustive Concordance of the Bible:[48]

Hebrew Words

1. **Chiwl,** (Khool) (2342) – To twist or whirl in a circular or spiral manner. To travail in pain; fear.
   a. Judges 21:21
   b. Judges 21:23
   c. Psalms 96:9 (fear)
   d. Micah 4:10 (labor)

2. **Machowl,** (Maw—khole) (4234) – A round dance.
   a. Psalms 30:11
   b. Psalms 149:3
   c. Psalms 150:4
   d. Jeremiah 31:4
   e. Jeremiah 31:13
   f. Lamentations 5:15

3. **Mechowlah,** (Mekh—o—law) (4246) – A dance; company; dances.
   a.   Exodus 15:20
   b.   Exodus 32:19 (dance honoring a false god)
   c.   Judges 11:34
   d.   Judges 21:21
   e.   1 Samuel 18:6
   f.   1 Samuel 21:11
   g.   1 Samuel 29:5
   h.   Song of Solomon 6:13 (company)
   i.   Jeremiah 31:4

4. **Chagag,** (Kwaw—gag) (2287) – To move in a circle; to march in a sacred procession; to observe a festival.
   a.   Exodus 5:1
   b.   Exodus 12:14
   c.   Exodus 12:17
   d.   Exodus 23:14
   e.   Leviticus 23:41
   f.   Deuteronomy 16:15
   g.   Psalms 42:4

5. **Haliykah,** (Hal—ee—kaw) ((1979) – A walking caravan; procession; march.
   a.   Psalms 68:24–25

6. **Halal,** (Haw—lal) (1984) – To shine, boast, brag, foolish, to rave.
   a.   1 Chronicles 16:4, 10 glory), 25, 36
   b.   2 Chronicles 20:21
   c.   Ezra 3:10, 11
   d.   Psalms 26:17
   e.   Psalms 94:4
   f.   Psalms 145:3, 9
   g.   Psalms 150

7. **Yadah,** (Yaw—daw) (3034) – To worship with extended hands.
   a. Psalms 63:4
   b. 1 Chronicles 16:4 (thank)
   c. 1 Kings 8:33 (confess)
   d. Psalms 42:5, 107:8 (praise)

8. **Towdah,** (To—daw) (8426) – To extend the hands, adoration, a choir of worshippers, sacrifice.
   a. Nehemiah 12:31, 38, 40 (thanks)
   b. Psalms 26:7 (thanksgiving)
   c. Psalms 42:4 (praise)
   d. Psalms 50:14 (thanksgiving)
   e. Psalms 50:23 (praise)
   f. Psalms 107:22 (thanksgiving)
   g. Jeremiah 33:11 (praise)

9. **Giyl,** (Gheel) (1523) – To spin around under the influence of any violent emotion.
   a. As "Rejoice"—Psalms 2:11
   b. As "Joy"—Psalms 43:4
   c. As "Joyful"—Psalms 35:9
   d. As "Glad"—Psalms 31:7
   e. As "Gladness"—Joel 1:16
   f. As "Delight"—Proverbs 2:14

10. **Karar,** (Kaw—rar) (3769) – To dance.
   a. 2 Samuel 6:14 (dance)
   b. 2 Samuel 6:16 (dancing)

11. **Raqad,** (Raw—kad) (7540) – To stomp; to spring about wildly; to jump, leap or skip.
   a. 1 Chronicles 15:29 (dancing)
   b. Job 21:11 (dance)
   c. Psalms 29:6 (skip)
   d. Psalms 114:4, 6 (skipped)

e. Ecclesiastes 3:4 (dance)

f. Isaiah 13:21 (dance)

g. Joel 2:5 (leap)

h. Nahum 3:2 (jumping)

12. **Pazaz,** (Paw—zaz) (6339) – A strong leap or spring.

a. Genesis 49:24 (strong)

b. 2 Samuel 6:16 (leaping)

c. 1 Kings 10:18 (best)

13. **Alaz,** (Aw—laz) (5937) – To jump for joy triumphantly.

a. As "Rejoice"—Psalm 28:7

b. As "Joyful"—96:12

14. **Dalag,** (Daw—lag) (1801) – To spring or leap.

a. 2 Samuel 22:30

b. Psalms 18:29

c. Song of Solomon 2:8

d. Isaiah 35:6

e. Zephaniah 1:9

15. **Qaphats,** (Kaw—fats) (7092) – To draw together close; to leap by contracting the limbs; skip.

a. Song of Solomon 2:8 (skipping)

16. **Shiyr,** (Sheer) (7891) – To sing or the idea of strolling minstrelsy.

a. Exodus 15:21

b. 1 Chronicles 15:27

c. Psalms 33:3

d. Psalms 137:3

e. Jeremiah 20:13

Greek Words

1. **Agalliao,** (Ag—al—lee—ah) (G21) – Welcome; gladness; exceeding joy.
   a. As" Gladness"—Luke 1:14
   b. As "Joy"—Luke 1:44

2. **Hallomai,** (Hal—lom—ahee—) (242) – To jump, gush, leap or spring up.
   a. John 4:14 (springing)
   b. Acts 14:10 (leaped)

3. **Exallomai,** (Ex—al—lom—ahee) (1814) – To leap.
   a. Acts 3:8 (leaping)

4. **Skirtao,** (Skeer—tah—o)—(4640) – To jump; sympathetically move.
   a. Luke 1:41 (leap)
   b. Luke 1:44 (leaped)
   c. Luke 6:23 (leap)

5. **Orcheomai,** (Or—kheh—om—ahee) (3738) – To dance in a row or ring.
   a. Matthew 11:17
   b. Matthew 14:6 (wrong motives)
   c. Mark 6:22
   d. Luke 7:32

6. **Choros,** (Khor—os) (5525) – Round dance.
   a. Luke 15:25

7. **Prochoros,** (Prokh—or—os) (4402) – Listed as a Deacon of the early church; leader of the dance.

   a.   Acts 6:5

8. **Choregeo,** (Khor—ayg—eh—o (5524) – To be a dance leader; give; minister.

   a.   2 Corinthians 9:10 (minister)
   b.   1 Peter 4:11 (give, supply)

2

> For of him, and through him, and to him, are all things: to
> whom be glory forever. Amen.[1] ("Romans 11:36")

Everything was originally created to give glory to God. God loves
praise and especially music. God instructs us in Psalms 150 to praise
Him with the dance and with all kinds of instruments in the sanctuary. We were created for Him:

> For by him were all things created, that are in heaven, and
> that are in earth, visible and invisible, whether they be
> thrones, or dominions, or principalities, or powers: all things
> were created by him, and for him.[2] ("Colossians 1:16")

Dance was created by God to praise Him, but Satan took it and
duplicated it to the world and made it lustful and corrupt. Satan is
no creator; he is only out to pervert and steal God's creation. Satan
was originally created to praise and worship God in heaven. He
was made of tabrets, viles and pipes which made him be a living
orchestra:

> Thou hast been in Eden the garden of God; every pre-
> cious stone was thy covering, the sardius, topaz, and the

diamond, the beryl, the onyx, and the jasper, the sapphire, the emerald, and the carbuncle, and gold: the workmanship of thy tabrets and of thy pipes was prepared in thee in the day that thou wast created. Thou art the anointed cherub that covereth; and I have set thee so: thou wast upon the holy mountain of God; thou hast walked up and down in the midst of the stones of fire. Thou wast perfect in thy ways from the day that thou wast created, till iniquity was found in thee.[3] ("Ezekiel 28:13:15")

Satan was kicked out of heaven because of his pride. He wanted more glory than God. He is out to destroy what God created. Since God is the originator of everything, Satan tries to make people think that God has created bad things such as secular music, drugs and immoral sex. God created music for praise and worship for His glory; He created drugs, which were derived from plants and herbs for health and healing; and sex was created for reproduction and the intimate holy union between a man and a wife. Our most valuable gifts have been the targets of Satan's greatest perversions.

Dance, as we have known it in the world, has been functioning in areas outside of its original purpose. People see dance on MTV videos, commercials and movies done in a sexy or perverted way. That is why they are so uncomfortable when they are about to see it presented in church. They wonder what are the dancers going to wear, what type of music will be used or if the movements are going to make them think they are in the club. Dancers have to educate constantly the congregation with scriptures or narrations before the dance and not have a prideful spirit. It is not really the style of form or dance, but how the heart is operating. As long as the dance is ministering to people and not being done for self—gratification, people will get healed and delivered.

There are four reasons why God has created dance:

Purpose and Pleasure—The scripture clearly states God has created all things for His pleasure. In Psalms 149:4a, it says that the Lord takes pleasure in His people. He takes pleasure in the praise dance. The Bible also states in Ecclesiastes 3:1 that there is a time for every purpose under the heaven. There is a time to dance in the sanctuary to the glory of God.

> Thou art worthy, O Lord, to receive glory and honour and power: for thou hast created all things, and for thy pleasure they are and were created.[4] ("Revelation 4:11")

Fulfilling God's Purpose—It is God's purpose for his people to be set free by the truth of Jesus Christ and that they receive salvation. Through the message of the dance that can be fulfilled especially by bringing the scriptures to life. A drama or chore—drama dance could easily illustrate the meanings of the scriptures. John 8:32 says that when we know the truth, it will set us free. A dance has the same effect as a sermon; it sets people free. God tells us in Matthew 28:19 to go into all nations and tell that Jesus is Lord. We can preach it, sing it or dance it. It does not matter how we do it. Isaiah 61:1–2 tells us what the truth will do to people if we minister to them:

> The Spirit of the Lord God is upon me; because the Lord hath anointed me to preach good tidings unto the meek; he hath sent me to bind up the broken hearted, to proclaim liberty to the captives, and the opening of the prison to them that are bound; To proclaim the acceptable year of the Lord, and the day of vengeance of our God; to comfort all that mourn;[5] ("Isaiah 61:1–2")

Victory, Restoration and Celebration—Throughout the scripture, dance is strongly linked to freedom, life, restoration, salvation and victory over the enemy. Victory was shown in the first account in the Bible in Exodus 15 when Miriam celebrated with a tambourine dance after the Israelites crossed the Red Sea. Celebration was shown in the last account in the Bible in Luke 15 when the Prodigal Son returned home to music and dancing. Restoration was shown in the Bible in Jeremiah 30 and 31 as Israel was rebuilt after being in captivity:

> Again I will build thee, and thou shalt be built, O virgin of Israel: thou shalt again be adorned with thy tabrets, and shalt go forth in the dances of them that make merry.[6] ("Jeremiah 31:4")

Truth Restored—God wants all truths and their fundamentals to be restored to the Church, especially dance. He does not want his purpose to be misunderstood or perverted. The word tells us to study to show ourselves approved. We have to study the Word and know what God wants His people to know. Dance ministers should know the Word very well and be able to execute it through the dance so it can set people free, usher in the Holy Spirit and release salvation. Ephesians 6:13–14 tells us to put on our whole armor of God so that we can withstand the devil. If our armor is on, we can stand against the lies of the devil.

It is God's purpose for all things He has created to praise Him, bring pleasure to Him and know the truth so that when Jesus returns, we will not have a blemish, spot, wrinkle or be deceived.

Will of God for Us in Praise and Worship

The ultimate purpose for which God created us is to praise, thank and worship Him. These things are supposed to be done first as we enter into His gates and presence. Praise is a sacrifice and a choice from us to God even when we do not feel like it. Below are some praise scriptures that show that we were created to bring God glory:

> Rejoice evermore. Pray without ceasing. In everything give thanks: for this is the will of God in Christ Jesus concerning you.[7] ("1Thessalonians 5:16–18")

Enter into his gates with thanksgiving, and into his courts with praise: be thankful unto him, and bless his name.[8] ("Psalms 100:4")

Give unto the Lord the glory *due unto* his name: bring an offering, and come into his courts.[9] ("Psalms 96:8")

By him therefore let us offer the sacrifice of praise to God continually, that is, the fruit of *our* lips giving thanks to his name.[10] ("Hebrews 13:15")

This is why praise dancing has God's approval. It is like the dancers are cheerleaders for Him. Dancers jump, praise, shout, dance, flip and get excited over the victory of what He has done. Praise moves God. He is just like human beings. When we compliment someone, that person is nicer to us and will do more for us even if we do not ask. God does the same thing. He does even more for us when we compliment Him.

Here are some important facts on praise:
- Praise comes from a close relationship with God.
- To praise God totally, you must surrender your all.
- Praise is in the Bible 332 times and thanksgiving is in there 135 times.
- Praise is an Old Testament term and thanksgiving is a New Testament term.
- Praise brings healing and deliverance.
- Praise silences the devil.
- Praise brings salvation, strengthens faith and prepares us for miracles.
- God inhabits our praises.

Types of Praise

Non—Audible
- Lifting of hands
- Dancing
- Kneeling
- Meditating
- Sign Language
- Banners/Flags/Streamers

Audible
- Clapping
- Shouting
- Singing
- Instruments
- Stomping
- Tongues

Praise is what God has done and worship is the essence of who He is. It is His attributes. Worship is the intimate time believers have with God. When believers lose themselves and fall in love with God, worship will become natural and their constant state. In a love relationship, two people are so in love that they are just happy to hear the other person's voice, to spend quality time with them, to complement each other, or to tease with sweet nothings or nicknames. The time they spend together usually goes on for hours and they do not want it to end. This is an example of true worship and how God wants us to treat Him in our worship relationship. God seeks those who worship Him in spirit and truth:

> But the hour cometh, and now is, when the true worshippers shall worship the Father in spirit and in truth: for the Father seeketh such to worship him. God is a Spirit: and they that worship him must worship him in spirit.[11] ("John 4:23–24")

God definitely seeks dancers to praise and worship Him. Dancers are in His will and will have favor with Him because they are a vital advertising tool to lead others to Christ.

God's View of Dance

As stated before, God created us to praise and worship Him through the dance, preached word, singing, drama, with loud instruments, etc. Dance is a form of praise and whatever God created, it is good. In Zephaniah 3:17c, it states that God will "joy over us with singing." Joy in Hebrew means to dance or spin around. (Strong 1523–gil) The very origin of dance is with God, not with man. He joys over us with dance.

Exodus 5:1 states that after Moses and Aaron went in and asked Pharaoh to let the Israelites go, they suggested to him that they wanted to hold a *feast* (celebration). Every time the word feast is brought up in the Bible, it means a festival or celebration of food, dancing and music. This is the first indication of the type of worship God desired by His people. (Strong 2287–chaqaq; to move around in a circle)

Exodus 12:11 talks about eating and being merry during the Passover. Passover not only means salvation but to dance. (Strong 6452–pasah; to worship in a limping dance)

2 Corinthians 9:10 states "one that ministereth seed to the sower both minister bread for the food and multiplies the seed sown, which increases the fruits of righteousness." Ministereth means a leader that supplies all the necessary things for the ministry to go forth. They are sowing into the ministry for it to grow. (Strong 5524–choregeo; the leader of dance chorus) Our God sees His people as a dance group to be supplied with all its needs abundantly at His expense because He paid the price with the blood of Jesus.

As God ministers (choregeo) we should minister and be the leader of the dance group, furnish the dance group at our own expense and secure and supply all things necessary to fit out the dance group. God has entrusted us with the vision for dance in our church, district or country. His purpose is to call us to put ourselves out for others in prayer and intercession and to offer ourselves as a living sacrifice just as Jesus.

History of Dance in Church

While many individuals view dance in a worship service as new, others are aware that dance is found throughout the Bible. In fact, one can find references to movement and dance as far back as Genesis 1:1–3:

> In the beginning God created the heaven and the earth. And the earth was without form, and void; and darkness was upon the face of the deep. And the Spirit of God moved (hovered) upon the face of the waters. And God said, Let there be light: and there was light.[12] ("Genesis 1:1–3")

Verse 2 says that the Spirit of God "moved (hovered)" over the waters. To hover means to stretch out, in an attitude of covering, while slowly rocking or moving side—to—side or forward and back.[13] From the beginning, movement was important to God so much that He danced as He created and formed the Universe.

There are 27 occurrences of the English word "dance" and over 50 occurrences of Hebrew and Greek words in reference to an act or action that may be viewed as dance. Also, there are 12 observed acts of praise leading into worship. Of the 12, half of these acts are related to and action of the body through dance or movement. The liturgical dancer must understand the biblical and historical origin of dance as well as the significance of the movements. In this discovery, God will reveal the power and purpose He has always had for dance to stir up joy, deliverance, healing, warfare and worship.

Now let us look deeper into the history of dance in the church:

A.   For hundred of years, there was no separation of the dance from the world and church.

B.   331 AD—Constantine Era
   1.   All joyful dance ceases.
   2.   Art is coming back into the church.
   3.   Only spontaneous dance was left.
   4.   Only clergy led singing.
   5.   Sixteen hundred women led Gregorian chant in the church.

C.   Through the Dark Ages
   1. No dance was done in the church.

D.   900–11 AD
   1.   Minuet dances were done.
   2.   The body was considered evil; therefore, the body was covered up.

Now let us look at a deeper timeline of liturgical dance throughout the ages of the Hebrew's participation and view of it from a worship standpoint:

A.   The Hebrew people were a God—centered nation. Every area of their life was submitted to God by praying for their land, cattle, their coming in and going out. They sought the Lord for everything.

B.   The same was true in their worship. They worshipped and danced before the Ark, during festivals, after a victory or any time. Dance was a normal part of their everyday life. They did not view dance as carnal but as praising God.

C.   In the first five centuries of the Christian Church, dance was still acceptable because it was deeply planted in the soil of the Judeo—Christian tradition. Christians were accustomed to celebrating dance at worship and festivals because of the Hebrew tradition of dance.

D.   In two of the earliest Christian liturgies recorded in detail, dance was used in the order of service. It was perceived as one of the heavenly joys and part of the adoration of the divinity by the angels and the saved.

E.   In the early Middle Ages, many converts were turning to Jesus Christ and the focus of dance changed. The dance became sensual because new converts attempted to retain the dances of the pagan cults that they were previously executed. Because of this, many significant changes were made inside and outside of the church. The dance was tempered with warnings about its form by church leadership.

F.   After the fall of Rome, liturgical dance participation in the Mass became reserved for the clergy and was more restricted for the lay person. The clergy performed sacred dances for the congregation. The congregation under the guidance and approval of the church were allowed to dance certain sacred dances.

G.   It was in the latter part of the Middle Ages that dance began to suffer in the church due to dance manias and a surge called the Dance of Death. These dances came into existence due to the Black Plague which the church tried to suppress. Despite their attempts the popular dance persisted. The focus became the movement of the body instead of on the original meaning of the Christian dance was lost. During the Reformation dance was forced out of the church and into the secular realm.[14]

Jewish Dance—Main Dance in the Bible

Jewish dance was the main dance in the Bible. It goes back from Miriam to David and through the lineage of Jesus. It was very simple, repetitive and mostly done in a circle with clapping, stomping, twirling, singing, shouting, etc. (machowl—Strong 4234) It was done at festivals, the Passover, victory celebrations, feasts, and warfare battles.

The most popular type of Jewish dance used now in dance ministries is the Davidic dance. It is a physical expression of praise, thanksgiving and joy to Elohim (God). Some of the dances are patterned after traditional Israeli folk dances; others are originally choreographed by Messianic believers. Messianic believers are Jews who recognize that Yeshua (the original name of Jesus in Hebrew) is the promised Messiah who has come and will come again.[15] The dances are meant to be performed as a group without any emphasis on one dancer. The tone of the dances ranges from reverentially devotional to exuberantly joyful. Dancers include men, women, teenagers and young children. Some of the celebrations that include the Jewish dance are at b'nai mitzvots, weddings, Seders, and social gatherings. The dance is also appropriate for worship services because it unifies Jewish and Gentile believers in praising Adonai (the Lord).

An example of where a Jewish dance is performed is at a wedding. The Jewish wedding tradition is where the guests perform a circle dance around the bride and groom. The bride and groom may also be lifted above the circle. In some communities where dancing with opposite sex is prohibited, a special dance may be done where the dance partners hold opposite ends of a scarf.

Below are some Israeli folk dances[16]:

Hassidic—This dance was inspired by the early life of the prophets and was a presentation of spontaneous ecstasy to show inner exultation. It released the prophetic flow and brought the anointing of the Holy Spirit. The dancers did not sing words while they danced because they felt that words could not express what the heart felt so deeply.

Chassidim—A movement which originated among Polish Jews in the 18th century. They believed that sincere devotion and joy were acceptable to God and He should be served through joy rather than solemnity. The dances were done in a circle expressing equality. Every person represented a link in a chain without a beginning or end. Each person started with one hand or both resting on the shoulders of the person in front of them. The dance was accompanied by vocal songs.

Hora—This originated in Romania and typified the growth of new life in agriculture. It has now almost become the national dance of Israel. It expresses quality of life and intimate contact with the land. This dance is often done with clapping.

Debka—This dance had Oriental influence and was originally a dance of men linked in a row to express strength and self—confidence. It consisted of intricate footwork and had a war—like effect. It caused many to receive strength and to rise up to dance in power and might.

Yeminite—These movements were graceful and flowing with beautiful, prayerful arm and hand patterns. Beautifully embroidered handwork on the garments was a part of the culture, marked by the beauty of song and poetry. These dances were performed indoors in small crowded rooms, which allowed them to display strong vertical movements.

The Jewish dance is definitely ordained by God because Jews are the chosen people. In Genesis 15:1–5, God promised Abraham that he was going to have a son and bless his seed so that he would be able to number the generations to come. This was the Jewish lineage where David and Jesus had come. This is just one style of dance and fortunately we (the Gentiles) are a part of God's master plan of favor and salvation through Jesus Christ. All types of liturgical dance are accepted and loved by God.

Other People Who Danced in the Bible

When people refer to dance in the Bible, they always talk about David or Miriam. There were other people who danced in the Bible and played significant roles to praise, worship, mourn, celebrate, promote evil, warfare, etc. Some of them were children, women, men, armies, evil ones, animals and priests. Here are some examples of people who danced in the Bible:

Children —They send forth their little ones like a flock, and their *children* dance. They take the timbrel and harp, and rejoice at the sound of the organ.[17] ("Job 21:11–12")

But whereunto shall I liken this generation? It is like unto *children* sitting in the markets, and calling unto their fellows, And saying, We have piped unto you, and ye have not danced; we have mourned unto you, and ye have not lamented.[18] ("Matthew 11:16–17")

Women— And Jephthah came to Mixpeh unto his house, and, behold, his *daughter* came out to meet him with timbrels and with dances: and she *was his* only child; beside her he had neither son nor daughter.[19] ("Judges 11:34")

Therefore they commanded the children of Benjamin, saying, Go and lie in wait in the vineyards; And see, and, behold, if the *daughters* of Shiloh come out to dance in dances, then come ye out of the vineyards, and catch you every man his wife of the daughters of Shiloh, and go to the land of Benjamin.[20] ("Judges 21:20–21")

Men—And *David* danced before the Lord with all his might; and David was girded with a linen ephod.[21] ("2 Samuel 6:14")

Armies—And when he had consulted with the people, he appointed singers unto the Lord, and that should praise the beauty of holiness, as they went out before the *army*, and to say, Praise the Lord; for his mercy endureth for ever. And when they began to sing and to praise, the Lord set ambushments against the children of Ammon, Moab, and mount Seir, which were come against Judah; and they were smitten.[22] ("2 Chronicles 20:21–22")

Evil Ones—But when Herod's birthday was kept, the *daughter of Herodias* danced before them, and please Herod. Whereupon he promised with an oath to give her whatsoever she would ask. And she, being before instructed of her mother, said, Give me here John Baptist's head in a charger.[23] ("Matthew 14:6–8")

Animals—But wild beasts of the desert shall lie there; and their houses shall be full of doleful creatures; and owls shall dwell there, and *satyrs* shall dance there.[24] ("Isaiah 13:21")

Priests—So the *priests and the Levites* sanctified themselves to bring up the ark of the Lord God of Israel; And David spake to the chief of the Levites to appoint their brethren to be the singers with instruments of musick, psalteries and harps and cymbals, sounding, by lifting up the voice with joy.[25] ("1 Chronicles 15:14, 16")

Levels of Dance

There are three levels of dance in church that one might be called. Each is an important element of the body of Christ. In a church or dance ministry, there cannot be one without the other in order for the ministry to function properly and for God's purpose to be revealed in the service.

Congregational Dance—Everyone is called to this level. It is required for all of us to worship God and be on one accord. The Bible requires us to lift our hands in the sanctuary and praise Him with instruments, music and dance. The old saying is when praises go up, blessings come down. Once the atmosphere is set and the anointing is created by the Holy Spirit, the entire congregation is moved to break forth in worshiping in the dance. This same concept is similar to when the "spirit of prophecy" falls on a service, according to 1 Corinthians 14:31:

> For ye may all prophesy one by one, that all may learn, and all be comforted.[26] ("1 Corinthians 14:31")

Just like all can prophesy when the spirit falls down, all can dance. It does not matter who you are or what background you come from, all people are required in a worship service to lose themselves in the Lord.

The Gift of Dance—This is actually a God—given talent and ability to dance and because the "gifts and callings of God are without repentance" (Romans 11:29), a person with the gift of dance may either choose to use this in a secular environment or in the church. The emphasis here is on the "gift" or ability rather than the heart, attitude or calling.

Many people who have a natural gift to dance or who have learned how to dance well through lessons are not necessarily called to dance in a dance ministry or be used as a minister of dance. There is usually no anointing on it and the congregation perceives it as entertainment.

The Ministry or Office of Dance—There is no "Office of Dance" as there is the Office of the Prophet; however, there are those who are specifically called to minister in the dance. They are called Ministers of Dance. They not only have the gift to dance but have the gift to minister to the Lord and people. When they minister, it always results in souls being changed or saved.

Unbelief of Dance in the Church

Even though dance is all through the Bible in the Old Testament and New Testament, interpreted in Hebrew and Greek words, celebrated in Jewish biblical customs and is now spreading rapidly across the country and nations, it is not fully accepted in some places of worship.

Some religions, churches, pastors, ministers and spiritual officers do not know how God relates to dance or where dance is in the Bible. They can only relate to either David dancing with all of his might or where it says to praise the Lord with the dance in Psalms 149–150. They think that movement was for the Old Testament and not for now. They do not realize that dance is in the New Testament as well. They do not understand about God's original purpose of dance and how He is going to restore it back to the church. Some Christians and churches are getting the picture because they are studying more, see it on TV and attend conferences. It is mostly not received by other religions and denominations that are very conservative.

In preparing for this book, a small telephone survey was prepared for a couple of churches in various denominations and races in Memphis, Tennessee to see if they accepted liturgical dance in the church and how much they knew about the subject. Some of the findings were that this was a touchy subject, that pastors or ministers did not know a lot about dance in the Bible and that some religions do not relate dance to the Word and church. They might worship in a synagogue or mosque. If their religion did not use the Bible but used something else, they would not know what the Word said about dance.

The telephone survey asked ten questions and represented the denominations AME., Anglican, Apostolic, Assemblies of God, Association of Unity Churches, Baptist, Catholic, Church of Christ, Disciples of Christ, Muslim, Non—Denomination and Presbyterian. The efforts were unsuccessful in trying to reach Church of God In Christ, Jehovah Witness and Messianic Jews. The questions were:

1.   What is Liturgical Dance?

2.   Is Liturgical Dance a part of your church or denomination? If so, what type of dance or groups do you have?

3.   What do you think is God's view of Liturgical Dance in the church?

4.   What do you think is the universal church's view of Liturgical Dance?

5.   Despite your personal beliefs, why do you think Liturgical Dance is growing rapidly around the world?

6. Who was the first person that danced in the Bible?

7. What is the sole purpose of a dance ministry?

8. Do you see it as entertainment or ministry?

9. Can souls get saved through Liturgical Dance?

10. Is Liturgical Dance fully accepted in the church? (See Appendix Example #4)

Results

AME. Church—This was an African—American church that believed we were created to make God's praise glorious through body movements. They have an active praise dance team that ministers every Sunday. Occasionally, they do presentational dances. They have a male, female and children's group. They think that dance is God's standard through David. Dance is really big in their denomination, especially on the east coast. They believe that dance is moving rapidly because everyone is coming in the knowledge of praise and worship. The person who answered this survey did not know who the first person that danced in the Bible. They believe it is a ministry and that souls can get saved, but that dance is not fully accepted universally.

Anglican—They believe that dance is an attempt to illustrate attitudes and faith with music and movement. It is not a part of their church or denomination to their knowledge. They think God's view is that He focuses more on how much we worship and adore Him than on the form of expression. They felt that younger people seem to need more contemporary ways of worship. They believe David was the first to dance in the Bible. They believe that the sole purpose of a dance ministry is to glorify God and that it is hopefully a ministry. They doubt that dance can save souls alone and that it is not fully accepted in the church.

Apostolic—These were two different extreme opinions. Usually, apostolic churches are liberal, but one of the survey participants was very conservative. The conservative church did not know what liturgical dance was but admitted that their denomination accepts it. They believe that dance is related to worship and praise, but they think that it is for entertainment and souls cannot be saved from it. They do not believe that dance is fully accepted in the church.

The other church has an active dance group that ministers through prophetic, streamers, warfare, sign language, hip—hop and African. They think that dance pleases God and that He is restoring it back to the church. They believe that churches are doing dance because it is popular and that people do not fully understand it. They knew that Miriam was the first person to dance in the Bible. They believe that it brings about praise and worship, healing salvation and warfare. They know that it is a ministry but not completely accepted.

Assemblies of God—The church representing this denomination believes that liturgical dance is choreography to spiritual hymn songs. The type of dance they have at their church is the human video and their denomination accepts it at the national office. They incorporate it in their annual Fine Arts Festival. They believe that dance is appropriate and biblical as stated in Psalms 149 and 150. They admitted that dance is a touchy subject universally in the church but said that it is eye appealing and a form of evangelism that young people love. They said that the sole purpose of a dance ministry is to glorify God and that it is a ministry depending on who is leading it. They said that souls could get saved from liturgical dance if there is a conclusion or an altar call. They concluded that it is not fully accepted.

Association of Unity Churches—They believe that liturgical dance is praise through dance. They do not have a dance ministry but their denomination believes in it. Some of the other churches under this denomination use flags, banners and streamers. They see dance as a form of celebration and that it is very diverse. They think that it is more accepted because it is the 21st century and that people understand the Word more. They did not know who was the first person in the Bible. They said that the sole purpose of the dance ministry is for praise, it is a ministry, souls can get saved and it is accepted depending on the spiritual leader.

Baptist—These African—American churches believe that liturgical dance is an interpretation or expression of music and movement through dance. Two of them have dance ministries and the other one does not. They agreed that their denomination is involved with pantomime and a group of young people and women. They agreed that God accepts dance because David danced and Jesus danced in the temple. They agreed that universally some churches are caught up in tradition. Only one church knew that Miriam was the first person who danced in the Bible. The sole purpose of a dance ministry to them is for worship and praise. They summed it up by saying that it is a ministry and souls can get saved by dance. All three churches said that it is not fully accepted in the church.

Southern Baptist—This predominantly Caucasian based church believes that liturgical dance is an emotional time of dance from victory. They do not have a dance ministry, and they do more drama in their presentations. They think that God's view on dance is evil but joyous because He approved of David praising Him. They think that the universal church does not believe in it unless it is done during a presentation. They believe that it is growing rapidly because it is emotional. They thought that David was the first person who danced in the Bible. Even though they think that the sole purpose of dance is to glorify God, they still said that it was more for entertainment than ministry. At the end of the survey, they contradicted themselves by saying that souls can get saved and that it is fully accepted in the church.

Catholic—This African—American church defined liturgical dance as worship dance. They do have a dance ministry and feel that God approves it because of David dancing before the Ark of the Covenant. They did not know what the other denominations believed. They said that liturgical dance is growing because it helps people to lift their minds and hearts to God. They did not know who was the first person that danced in the Bible. They believe that dance brings forth praise and souls can get saved depending on the theology. They said that it is a ministry, and it is fully accepted in the church.

Church of Christ—Three churches in this faith were not familiar with liturgical dance so, they did not have a definition. They did not know what God's view or the universal church's view since they did not know what liturgical dance was. They did not know that it was growing rapidly around the world, but they guessed it was because dance attracts attention. One church knew that Miriam was the first to dance in the Bible, one said David and one did not know. They thought the soul purpose of dance is to entertain and that souls cannot get saved by dance and that it is not fully accepted.

Disciples of Christ—One was African—American and the other was Caucasian. They said that liturgical dance is spiritual worship and dance based liturgy. One church had a dance ministry with a wide range of types of dance and other did not have one. They believed that dance is a part of their denomination. They feel that God approves it because David danced and that the universal church is beginning to accept it more. One church said that it is growing rapidly because it is liberty in the Word and the other said that people enjoy this kind of open expression. One knew that Miriam was the first person who danced in the Bible but the other one guessed David. One church could not finish the survey. The other finished by saying the sole purpose of a dance ministry is to reach people for Christ, it is a ministry, probably souls can get saved and it is not fully accepted in the church.

Muslim—They said that liturgical dance is a dance that represents the religious culture. They do not have dance in their mosques and do not know what is God's view on dance in the church. When asked about the universal church's view on liturgical dance, they said that the Christian Bible and their books say the same thing. It is up to the individual religion to incorporate it. They did not know why dance is growing, who was the first person to dance in the Bible or what the sole purpose of it is. They did say that it is considered a ministry and that they think that souls can get saved by it. They concluded that dance is not fully accepted.

Non—Denominational—These churches said that liturgical dance is a dramatic way of worship that gives God glory through rhythmic movement. All of them have dance groups at their church specializing in streamers, flags, hip—hop, mime and praise dance. They said that God is pleased with dance and that it is another form of worship. They said the universal church's view is mixed because of tradition, but some push it for the youth to be involved. One church said that it is growing rapidly because praise defeats the enemy. The other ones said that it is different and attracts the youth. One church knew that Miriam was the first person to dance in the Bible and the other ones said David. They said that the sole purpose is to minister through exaltation, joy and praise and to create a spirit of unity. All of the churches said that dance is a ministry. Three of them said that souls can get saved by it and one had not seen it done. All agreed that it is not fully accepted in the church.

Presbyterian—They did not know what liturgical dance is, so they guessed that it is a religious dance. They do not have a dance ministry. They think that God's view of it is prudent, had no idea on what the universal church's view is and did not know that it was growing rapidly around the world. They did not know who the first person that danced in the Bible. They did admit that the sole purpose of a dance ministry is the artistic expression of God's love and that it is a ministry. They did not think that souls can get saved by it and that some people have accepted dance in the church.

Other denominations—Attempts were made to other denominations such as Church of God in Christ, Jewish and Jehovah Witness. One said that they were not interested in assisting with the survey, no one answered the telephone at two of them and the line was busy at the other.

After looking at these surveys from a couple of churches per denomination, most of them did not understand the place of the dance in the Bible and God's view. It was obvious that they have not studied a lot in the area of dance. Eighty percent of the churches surveyed believed that dance is not fully accepted, ten percent believed that it depends on the church and ten percent believed that it was fully accepted.

Restoration of the Dance

God is pouring out His spirit all over the world on dance ministries. It is His will to bring back the dance and praise the way it was illustrated in the Bible and in the Jewish culture. It is His purpose for us to praise Him through dance, song, worship and preached word for the future generations. The Holy Spirit and revelation of knowledge are being poured out to the body of Christ as never before. There is a unity among the brethren that surpasses any previous move of God.

> This shall be written for the generation to come: and the people which shall be created shall praise the Lord.[27] ("Psalms 102:18")

Jesus instructs us in Matthew 28:19–20 to go into *all* nations and tell that Jesus is Lord. Then in Psalms 117 tells us to praise the Lord *all* nations and *all* people. In the last days *all* people will praise him with the dance. God promised that the Tabernacle of David was going to be restored. King David instituted a brand new order of worship in his day by placing the Ark of the Covenant in a new tabernacle on Mt.

Zion and by ordaining a new priesthood of singers and musicians to worship and praise the Lord before the Ark continually.

> In that day will I raise up the tabernacle of David that is fallen, and close up the breaches thereof; and I will raise up his ruins, and I will build it as in the days of old:[28] ("Amos 9:11")

David was a man after God's own heart because he loved to praise God with the dance. God was pleased with the Ark and that generation of "praisers". He tells us in Jeremiah 31:4,13 that He will rebuild Israel and again the maidens shall be adorned with tambourines and go forth in the dance and rejoice. Also, He said that young men and old men together will rejoice in the dance.

Today various revival movements have inspired the renewal and acceptance of dance within the worship life of the church. The rich biblical foundation and tradition of dance is encouraging congregations and individuals to be free in expressive worship once again. Therefore, *all* things will be restored unto God in these last days.

> And he shall send Jesus Christ, which before was preached unto you: Whom the heaven must receive until the times of restitution of all things, which God hath spoken by the mouth of all his holy prophets since the world began.[29] ("Acts 3:20–21")

3

HOW TO START A DANCE MINISTRY

Dance ministries are popping up all over the world now. Some are for show and performance, some are used as a vehicle to get the youth involved and some are truly for ministry. As more conferences, workshops and outreach groups are developing, more dance ministries are understanding their purpose in the kingdom of God. They know that there is a place for them in the church. They are implementing symbols, praise garments, colors and scriptures into their dance presentations.

Some pastors start dance ministries and appoint a person they feel can work with the youth or who would not mind adding something else to his or her plate. This might result in a person leading the ministry with no knowledge of dance or Biblical understanding of how God wants a dance ministry to operate. The pastor is looking at the leadership skills of that person or the availability. This is the wrong way to start a ministry that is responsible for saving souls.

A dance ministry should be birthed through intercession. Through this process the Holy Spirit will lead how to do it and who to use. Depending on the mandate and denomination of the church involved, that is the way the doctrines, rules and requirements should be set. If it is a charismatic church, the ministry will operate fully like the model church in Acts 2 and allow the gifts to flow and represent all chapters of the Bible regarding dance as stated in the previous chapters. The different types of dance can be fully displayed such as praise, worship, prophetic, flags, banners, streamers, warfare, congregational, etc. If the church is of a certain denomination, then the ministry will operate in a box and abide by the rules of that church not realizing the fullness and potential of the ministry. That is why the Bible tells us to "study to show thyself approved." When we study the Old Testament, the New Testament, Hebrew and Greek Translations and Biblical cultures, then the dance ministry can function the way God originally created it to function.

What is a Dance Ministry?

A dance ministry is a group of dancers and ministers who minister dance in a church or public place with the intent of leading people to Christ through many dance forms, drama, spoken word or music. It could be two people, or it could be 200 hundred people in the ministry. There is a church in New York with actually 200 members. They have one leader, an assistant, seven choreographers and different groups within the 200 members. They have a children's group, a praise team, a dance choir, a men's group, an older women's group and an outreach group and network. They have three services and different groups minister a month or for a particular service on a rotational basis.

For any ministry, there should be a developmental Biblical or skill period before one can join, even after the dancers have accepted their call. Some churches make a three—rehearsal requirement or even a three—month period before the members can start ministering with the group. Just like churches require new members to attend new member classes for a couple of months before they can join a ministry, the dance ministry should do the same.

How to Recognize the Call to Dance Ministry

Everyone is not called to be in a dance ministry. Most people want to join the dance ministry because they either like to dance, were really ministered to by the ministry, have taken dance lessons, can dance really well, want to put their child in it for show; want to get their child involved, want a baby sitting service, think they have to join a ministry so this one fits closely to their gift, or they see it prospering and want to be a part. These reasons do not have anything to do with their call (See Appendix Example #5).

A call speaks to a burden or a passion to do something or for something. The central focus of the call of the liturgical dancer is the deep desire to see the souls of the people and nations saved and lives changed through the power and anointing of the dancer. God calls everyone at the time of conception when they were in their mother's womb.

> Before I formed thee in the belly I knew thee; and before
> thou camest forth out of the womb I sanctified thee, and I
> ordained thee a prophet unto the nations.[1] ("Jeremiah 1:5")

In his mother's womb, Jeremiah was called to be a prophet to the nations. The dancer's call is ordained by God before they were born. Usually, whatever a person's natural gift is that they used for the world is the gift that God ordained them in the womb for only His glory. Their call is something they love to do all of the time even when they do not feel like it or even if they do not get paid. It is their passion. Sometimes we get sidetracked and off course of our purpose. Unfortunately, one is able to recognize their call if they are always attacked in a certain area. A dancer might get attacked by Satan over and over through injuries so that they cannot fulfill their purpose of dance. This is a trick and might be a distraction, but if God has called that person, he or she is going to overcome every attack and fulfill their call. God might have to call and remind a person several times before he or she recognizes His voice and accepts his or her calling just like Samuel did.

And the Lord called Samuel again the third time. And he arose and went Eli, and said, Here am I; for thou didst call me. And Eli perceived that the Lord had called the child. Therefore, Eli said unto Samuel, Go, lie down: and it shall be, if he call thee, that thou shalt say, Speak, Lord; for thy servant heareth. So Samuel went and lay down in his place. And the Lord came, and stood, and called as at other times, Samuel, Samuel. Then Samuel answered, Speak; for thy servant heareth.[2] ("1 Samuel 3:8–10")

Five—Fold Ministry

Once dancers accept their call to dance ministry, they have to know what specific area of dance ministry they have been called. Jesus established a structure of ministry gifts for the Body of Christ to follow in Ephesians 4:11–13:

And he gave some, apostles; and some, prophets; and some, evangelists; and some, pastors and teachers; For the perfecting of the saints, for the work of the ministry, for the edifying of the body of Christ: Till we all come in the unity of the faith, and to the knowledge of the Son of God, unto a perfect man, unto the measure of the stature of the fullness of Christ:[3] ("Ephesians 4:11–13")

Every person called to ministry works within this God—given framework. Even though dancers are worshippers, they have a different mission, purpose, and assignment given to them by God. Once they understand their office or their ministry gift, an inner liberation will occur and they will be released to flow in their gift supernaturally by the Holy Spirit. Dancers can have a dominant gift which is the one they are compelled to do successfully, but they still have other gifts under the five—fold ministry. God might have positioned a dancer at a certain church for the very purpose of revolutionizing the worship experience through dance; so the dancer should be clear of his or her call and ministry gift. Listed below are the five ministry gifts and their characteristics:

The Apostolic Dancer—This is the first ministry gift. These people are sent by God with the task of starting and overseeing churches. Therefore, the apostolic dancer is one who is "sent forth" to birth new and unique ministries across the world, while serving as a spiritual guide to the leaders of those ministries. He or she must have a broad, global vision of their calling to the entire world. Some other characteristics are:

- Nations—minded
- Trains leaders and has a true heart for leaders
- Disciplined in his/her personal affairs
- Operates according to protocol, order, and consideration of impact to others
- Anointed with supernatural wisdom and keen insight to discern the motives of others
- Skilled in conflict—resolution and reconciliation as it relates to individuals and/or groups
- Excellent management skills

The Prophetic Dancer—A prophet is one who boldly speaks forth and openly proclaims divine messages or revelations from the Lord. These messages come by the Holy Spirit and may manifest through dreams, visions, word of knowledge, word of wisdom, interpretation of tongues or some other unctions of the Holy Spirit. Thus, the prophetic dancer is one anointed to bring forth and openly proclaim these messages with his or her body. He or she is able to interpret the Word of God through movement spontaneously give to him or her as the Holy Spirit gives utterance. Some characteristics are:

- He or she is an intercessor
- Possesses supernatural gifts of discernment, interpretation of tongues, and interpretation of dreams
- Will move and act spontaneously according to the leading of the Holy Spirit
- Actively engages himself or herself in spiritual warfare through dance

- Has a strong sense of integrity/truth in personal affairs and in movement interpretation
- Carries an anointing to pull down strongholds and bring about deliverance in spoken word or dance

The Dance Evangelist—An evangelist has a deep burden and desire to bring lost souls to Jesus Christ. The dance evangelist will always seek to manifest the fact that "God so loved the world that He gave His only begotten Son, and whosoever would believe in Him shall not perish, but have everlasting life" (John 3:16). Therefore, this type of dancer will have to strive to minister in a way that convinces and convicts persons of their sins, thus bringing them to repentance. Some characteristics are:

- Has an unusual burden to travel throughout the world
- Very radical and innovative in his or her approach to soul winning
- Strong compassion for the poor and underprivileged
- Called to minister outside the church such as prison, street ministry, hospitals, etc.
- Anointed to bring persons to repentance
- Possesses the ability to travail in his or her dance until a breakthrough occurs

The Dance Pastor and Teacher—A pastor is one who is responsible for overseeing the spiritual welfare of believers. A pastor must also have the ability and anointing of a teacher. Teachers are those who have special gifts and abilities to teach, explain and expound on the Word of God. For the Dance Pastor/Teacher is responsible for discipleship, teaching and accountability. They understand the importance of living a holy life and being consecrated before the Lord. These are usually the leaders or directors of dance ministries. These persons are able to discern, identify and nurture the spiritual growth of their dancers based on their observations and inter—actions with their members. These observations may occur through group prayer, devotional time, group Bible study, church attendance and the level of anointing operating in that person's dance ministry overall. Some characteristics are:

- Possesses the heart of a servant
- Sincere compassion and love for people
- Called to teach children and youth; does so effectively and joyously
- Possesses the heart of a shepherd
- Supernatural wisdom and keen discernment of the needs of people
- Anointed with a magnetic personality
- Extremely organized and detail—oriented

Once a person recognizes his or her call and understands how each ministry gift functions, he or she can pray to see if they will be able to meet the requirements of either a leader or a team member.

Requirements of a Dance Ministry Leader

Once the dance ministry has been established, a leader should be appointed by God. The pastor and leaders of the church should fast and pray to seek God on who He wants to be in charge of this anointed ministry. A leader or Minister of Dance should meet the following requirements:

- Know that he or she is responsible and held accountable for what the ministry does.
- Pray, meditate and ask God who should be in the ministry and what message He wants to convey to His people through the music, praise garments, colors, type of dance, etc.
- Must establish rules and guidelines for the dancers and class participation.
- Must audition and interview interested dancers before they can join the ministry.
- Must be able to work and flow well with the pastor and minister of music.
- Has been proven faithful in the church.

- Has the heart of a servant.
- Share the vision of the church and will not bring division.
- Be skillful in dance and in the spiritual realm.
- Be able to choreograph different styles and levels of dance after being led by the Holy Spirit.
- Be able to release the dancers into ministry by laying hands on them to impart the anointing and prophesying over their life—giving direction concerning the ministry.
- Be able to lead the dancers in Bible study, prayer, fasting, etc.
- Be organized, administrative and disciplined.
- Must have a teachable and humble spirit.
- Be able to lead the congregation into becoming worshippers.
- Must be able to work hard, have a vision and a vision for the ministry.
- Must not waiver after God has told him or her to do something concerning the ministry even if other people or leaders tell him or her otherwise.

God has to appoint a leader because a good dancer might not be the best leader or the best administrative person might not be able to dance well. The leader needs to be well versed and able to take criticism and be scrutinized. The leader can not be a weak person because most things that happen concerning the ministry are not personal. Sometimes, the leader might have to put personal money or extra time in the ministry. This position is not for everyone, but God knows who He wants to lead His ministry.

Requirements of the Members of a Dance Ministry

There should be certain requirements a member should understand before he or she joins the ministry. In most churches, people look at it as something to do for fun and not as a ministry serving God and bringing people to Christ. Below are the requirements for a member of a dance ministry:

- Has a burden for intercession
- Knows how to press in until a breakthrough comes
- Has God's purpose and the church's purpose in mind—not his or her agenda
- Knows how to submit to authority
- Knows how to promote unity in the Body of Christ
- Willing to learn
- Skillful in dance
- If he/she is an excellent dancer, willing to help the leader in any way possible
- Able to follow dress codes, dance schedules and rehearsal times
- Enrolled in a Bible Study
- Be a member of the church involved
- Be consistent and dedicated
- Has a humble, but confident spirit
- Be flexible
- Be focused before ministering by going to a quiet place alone to meditate, warm—up and rehearsing
- Go the extra mile by studying parallel scriptures, working out in other sports, attending workshops, participating in other productions, renting movies or going to plays that are related to the character portrayed or meditating on the music

Being a part of a dance ministry is a serious decision for spiritually mature people who really want to minister unto the Lord with excellence. God wants our best. He is a jealous God. He does not like it when we do all of our secular activities better than kingdom activities like cheerleading or basketball. The Word tells us to "seek ye first the kingdom of God" in (Matthew 7:33). A potential member of a dance ministry should really seek God to see if this is in His perfect will for him or her to be in this type of ministry no matter how skilled they might appear. This thought leads to the next question below.

Should Children Be in a Dance Ministry?

This is an issue that is universal among dance ministries all over the world. Some ministries accept children and some do not. Most churches separate the groups such as the children's team, the youth team and the adult team. Even though the Bible cites instances of children dancing in Matthew 11:16–17 and Job 21:11–12, some ministry leaders feel that they are not spiritually mature enough to win souls and conduct warfare. They feel unless the children are like Samuel and are serious about the things of God, they should not be part of the permanent dance team. These children should have parents or adults who will take the responsibility of interceding for them because they will be seriously attacked by the enemy. The singers, musicians and dancers go ahead of the army, and they are attacked first (Psalms 68:25). Most members of dance ministries are adults and might let special children participate once they reach the age of 12. They still might be allowed to participate in special occasions. The leader should be in constant prayer to see if God wants to use a special child. There are some exceptions.

Our church allows children in the dance ministry. We have an all—inclusive ministry including children, youth and adults. Most times they dance together, but every once in a while they dance separately. They have to audition, write an essay on their relationship with God, attend Bible study during dance ministry, attend praise and worship conferences and workshops, and fast and pray at all times during the ministry. If God ordains it, children can be allowed.

Ministry Staffing: Artistic vs. Administrative

The ministry should have other people or committees to assist the leader/director to make it run smoothly. Most churches have a Creative and Arts Ministry which includes dance, music, media, and pageantry (banners) are all under one unit. They work together especially if the church is producing a major production for Easter or Christmas. There is usually an Artistic Staff and Administrative Staff.

Artistic Staff:

Director—This person leads, guides and directs the overall spiritual formation, creative, and technical aspects of the Arts Ministry. He or she is responsible for the spiritual growth, development and general welfare of the members.

Assistant Director—This individual is responsible for leading the ministry team in every capacity as needed in the absence of the Director. He or she should serve as the key intercessor for the Director or team and should be the key coordinator for special conferences, seminars and workshops hosted by the ministry team or hosted for his or her further enrichment.

Worship Leader—This person is responsible for opening every meeting, rehearsal or gathering time of devotion. This may be done through prayer, song, intercession, sharing or however the Holy Spirit leads. He or she should meet with the Director to see what Bible study or special topics to be covered during meeting times.

Choreographer—This person must stay on the cutting edge of what is happening in the world now. He or she must work closely with the Director and Assistant in order to maintain the overall vision that God has set for the team. Also, he or she must be able to create dances, plays or chore—dramas and should have technique and be an excellent, called, anointed communicator and teacher.

Praise Garment Designer/Seamstress—They must be born again and spirit filled as described in Exodus 28:2–3. They must be highly skilled and full of wisdom in order to create garments that are glorious and praise worthy to the Lord. They must be able to work closely with the Director to capture the vision and able to be both culturally and Kingdom—relevant in their creations. They must be familiar with the choreographic repertoire of the team. This will assist in making wise decisions regarding specific costuming and fabrics that will enhance the ministry presentation.

Audio Engineer—This individual should be skilled and trained in various aspects of sound engineering and technology. This person must work closely with the Directors and the Choreographers to stay abreast of the kinds and types of music required and all necessary aspects of the dance or dramatic ministry presentations that require sound effects. He or she should know all of the proper cuing of CDs or cassettes at the appointed time. This role is critical to the success of the ministry team because the audio engineers must be equipped and able to take authority in the spirit realm over all manner of technical difficulties, power outages, and equipment trouble during times of ministry.

Administrative Staff:

Lead Administrator—This person is responsible for all administrative functions for the ministry team. He or she works closely with the directors to ensure that overall organization, assimilation, and distribution of information to the team is executed. He or she coordinates with the director administratively in regards to ministry engagements and logistics such as transportation, accommodations, etc. He or she serves as an administrative assistant to the director.

Marketing/Events Coordinator—This person is responsible for promoting the ministry team in a godly and excellent fashion throughout the community, city or abroad. He or she should seek out opportunities to minister in various arenas and venues. He or she should keep the ministry abreast of functions, seminars, conferences, etc.

Parent Core Committee—This team of parents assists the ministry when children are involved. It assists with costume changes, sewing, discipline, fundraisers, recruitment, etc. If the ministry travels, it assists as chaperones.

Finance Administrator—This person establishes and maintains accounting records for the team through banking and excellent stewardship. He or she ensures proper procedures are maintained with regards to intake and distribution, seeks out opportunities to invest in other ministries and charitable organizations and pays all ministry team bills/obligations. He or she also makes sure that the ministry team pays a regular tithe to the church under which they are covered.

Fundraising Representatives—These representatives plan and supervise activities and events that will serve to bring in and generate income to the ministry teams' general fund. From the initial concept to its completion, these persons will develop creative, innovative ways to generate income for the sustaining, welfare, and advancement of the ministry.

Depending on the size of the ministry, all of these administrative and artistic positions are not necessary. However, in the planning stages, it is good to have established guidelines and more zeal and excellence than that of any secular organization. These positions should be viewed as our "worship" offered unto God as well. God requires that everything should be done in a decent and orderly way. If dance ministries follow this guiding principle, glory will be brought to the Father.

Registration and Audition Requirements

Now it is time to establish the foundation, the rules and the guidelines of the dance ministry. Each church will be different, but there should be a consistent order for the dancers to follow. The next couple of sections of this book will be step—by—step instructions on how our dance ministry operates at Mississippi Boulevard Christian Church in Memphis, Tennessee. After years of experience in the professional dance world, prayer, meditation, studying the scriptures, attending and facilitating workshops and extensive travel, this is how God instructed me to lead the dance ministry at our church from 1990 to present.

Registration and Sign—ups—Instead of taking new people every month or quarterly, we take new dancers once a year. An announcement is advertised in the church bulletin and on the video screens during worship service a couple of weeks before registration. Sometimes, we ask one of the ministers to make the announcement in the pulpit. Since we have a large church, we have registration every fall during the Bible and Ministry Fair. All of the ministries and Bible study classes set—up a table in the Fellowship Hall after church to encourage people to sign—up (See Appendix Example #6).

Sign—Up Table—The ministry leader, a few officers, parents and dancers take turns sitting at the table. Sometimes, cute younger dancers showcase their dance outfit while they walk around and ask people to come to the table. Located on the table are the dance ministry sign (See Appendix Example #7), the requirement flyer (See Appendix Example #8), the sign—up sheet (See Appendix Example #9), the registration form (See Appendix Example #10), the audition/workshop schedule (See Appendix Example #11) and the audition sign—up time sheet (See Appendix Example #12).

Requirements—In order to join our ministry, one has to meet the following requirements:

- Be a baptized believer and member of our church
- Be active in a Bible Study and pursuing a worship relationship with God
- Be experienced in dance/acting/signing/tumbling
- Be at least 8 years old to adult
- Must prepare a 32—count dance routine
- Must write a two—paragraph statement on their relationship with God and how they are going to incorporate it in the ministry
- Be required to attend a series of preparatory workshops before they are released to minister

We also advertise that the ministry needs seamstresses, costume designers, stage/prop/worship production assistants, artists and sign designers, narrators, computer and administrative assistants, prayer warriors, devotion leaders and sponsors and fundraisers. This lets people know that there is a place for them in the church for them to be able to use their gifts, especially if they think they have to dance to be in the dance ministry.

Registration Form—We used to have a general sign—up sheet with the name, address, parent's name, telephone number, e—mail address, age status and the area and years of training. Now they have to fill out an extensive registration form that includes the above personal information, emergency contact information, audition requirements, insurance information, gender and several questions about how they would benefit from being in the ministry and how the ministry would benefit from them being a part.

Audition Schedule—Potential members have to be able to come to the auditions. They have 10 minutes and are rated on technique, personality, material selected, anointing, and their essay. This process is done not to scare off potential members, but to show them how serious it is to minister and to see their level of technique and skill. Usually, the minister of dance or leader selects everyone, even the beginners. Once they have been selected, the new members have to attend several dance ministry workshops with their parents, start reading an assigned book, take an exam (if decided by leader) and purchase their praise garments before they can minister. This may take about a month and a half to complete.

Ministry Guidelines

Every dance ministry should have guidelines for the group and parents to follow. Since our ministry is 85% children, there has to be rules for them to follow, especially for parents. Sometimes parents are the ones who do not comply with the ministry because they want to do it their way. For the child's secular activities such as cheerleading, they follow every rule and pay on time. For church activities they are slack and do whatever they want. Also, adult members do not think they have to comply with rules because they are grown. God expects excellence and order for His ministry. He is a jealous God! People always want Him to bless them, their ministry and their personal life, but they do not want to do it His way and form a relationship with him. Below are some of the areas that are discussed in our guidelines in which at the end, the parents have to sign and turn in to the ministry leader (See Appendix Example #13 for complete sheet):

- Minister of Dance contact information
- Church information
- Operational months of ministry
- Praise garment (costumes) responsibilities and location of stores
- Class format
- Assigned book information
- Expectations
- Officer information
- Demerit System and Progress Report Information
- Attendance policy
- Hours and class time information
- Orientation workshop and audition information
- Conference, retreat and concert information
- Praise garment and prop fee
- Fundraising information
- Fasting requirements
- Day of worship service or event requirements
- Tear off signature portion

Once the parents or members have read the guidelines and rules, they are to sign the bottom portion, tear it off and return it to the ministry leader.

Permission Form—Sometimes if the ministry is going on a trip or is having a retreat, there is a separate permission form that needs to be completed. This will be discussed in detail later in Chapter Six.

Electing Officers

Our ministry just implemented this recently. For 14 years as the ministry leader, I had been doing every single administrative and artistic element for the ministry. For the past three years, parents have been helping more with the costumes, sewing and being on the telephone committee. Some of the students were assigned to be dance captains. Participants of the ministry need to be used in their other gifts. This will allow them to feel that they are a part, needed and will increase their loyalty to the ministry. The leader should remind them that it is their ministry as well, not the leader's ministry. This will also cut down on jealousy what they might have toward the leader. Our ministry has the following officers:

Minister of Dance/Choreographer—This is the director/leader and main choreographer of the group. All final decisions come from this person. Most of the devotions, prayers, requests, and class format are enforced by her/him.

Assistant Director—This person is not necessarily a dancer, but it is the director's right hand. They are in the lead when the director is absent, attend church and staff meetings with or without the director, occasionally conducts Bible study and assists with the decisions for the ministry.

Secretary—This person is responsible for the telephone calls, administrative work, prayer requests, praise reports, minutes from the meetings, trip/conference/retreat information and other duties assigned by the director.

Treasurer—This person is responsible for collecting dues, trip and fundraising monies, conference registrations and meeting other financial obligations for the ministry as delegated by the director.

Praise Garment Committee Representative—This person represents the praise garment (costume) committee in making final decisions about what the dancers are going to wear after the vision from the director has been shared. They attend the meetings, suggest fabric samples and give suggestions to the director.

Fundraising Representative—This person is responsible for giving to the director possible fundraising ideas for the ministry.

Parent Representative—This person represents the parents. They coordinate how the parents are going to assist with changing of praise garments/props during services, concert or ministry engagements. They also are a voice for the parents when decisions are about to be made concerning the children.

Adult Dance Captain—This person represents the adults and assists with leading the class during warm—ups and teaching choreography in the director's absence.

Youth Dance Captain—This person represents the teenagers and assists with leading the class during warm—ups and teaching choreography in the director's absence.

Children's Dance Captain—This person represents the children and assists with leading the class during warm—ups and teaching choreography in the director's absence.

During the first year, the leader will choose the officers based on God's leading, commitment, talent, skill level and walk with God. The officers will be voted on and chosen by the ministry members after the first year.

Creating a Roll, Telephone Roster, Demerit System and Progress Reports

If a ministry is large and has a lot of children, there should be a system set—up where the leader can keep up with the members. Because the ministry is in a church, some members and parents take advantage of the rules and do not follow them. For secular, work or school activities, they follow without a problem. For church, they sometimes break the rules. Most young people are in two to three ministries, school activities, etc. This means that there are going to be conflicts, absences and tardies. My ministry members will not tell me all of the time what is going on, so I had to implement a system that everyone can follow.

Roll—If a member misses two consecutive rehearsals without informing me, those are considered unexcused absences. All they have to do is call me to let me know that they will not be there. When they have two unexcused absences, they have to make up three consecutive rehearsals. All of their participation, absences and tardies are recorded on a formal roll (See Appendix Example #14).

Telephone Roster—This can be something simple that has member information for the purpose of mailing or calling them about new information. It has the member's name, parent's name, home address, E-mail address and telephone number (See Appendix Example #15).

Demerit System—This is something new that we have implemented. Since some dancers have taken advantage of the ministry and have not abided by all of the rules, we have created a demerit system that keeps up with everything the dancers do. If they have received five demerits, they will be asked to sit down from the ministry for a period of time until the leader decides when they can return (See Appendix Example #16). The number five was chosen because five represents grace. Some of the reasons for a dancer to receive a demerit are:

- Lateness
- Unexcused Absences
- Gum Chewing
- Excessive Talking During Class
- Attitude
- Excessive Talking Before/During Service
- Disrespect to Assigned Leader

- Does Not Know Dance After Weeks of Practice
- Not Turning Forms/Money On Time
- No Ballet Shoes/Hair Not in Bun/Wearing Earrings
- Does Not Have Bible/Book/Paper/Pen

Progress Reports—From time to time, the parents/members are kept abreast of how well they are doing in the ministry. This tool can be used as encouragement or to let them know of their areas of development (See Appendix Example #17). The areas that are on the progress report are:

- Attendance
- Attitude
- Ability to Catch on to Dances/Assignments:
- Participation in Bible Study
- Ministry Growth
- Technique Growth
- Focus
- Cooperation
- Assigned Tasks in a Timely Manner
- Participation in Outside Events

Class Format

Each dance ministry class or rehearsal should have a format with a combination of spiritual, physical and creative components. The components to our rehearsals are prayer requests/praise reports, Bible study/book review, warm—ups, learning dance combinations to the planned dances, announcements and closing prayer. Let us look at some of these components below:

Prayer/Praise Reports—Start the rehearsal with soft worship music while they are arriving and right before they are to pray. Have them close their eyes while listening to the music and start to write down their prayer requests and praise reports on the form (See Appendix Example #18). When the music is finished, ask for them to tell their prayer requests and praise reports. Start the prayer and let the Holy Spirit lead.

Bible Study/Book Review—Generally, study chapters that relate to the dance and song the ministry is using for the next worship service or ministry engagement. If there is a theme or an advanced sermon title, look up those scriptures so the dancers will have a full understanding of the dance and what it means. The dance needs to minister to the dancers first, and then they will be able to minister to the congregation effectively (See Appendix Example #19/20).

Sometimes the leader can assign dance ministry books to his or her ministry and have them read a chapter a week and go over some questions related to the chapter. After the dancers have read the whole book and have answered all of the questions on the handouts, the leader can give them a quiz or test on the entire assigned book (See Appendix Example #21/22).

Warm—ups—The leader has the dancers go through a complete aerobic, stretching, strengthening and cardiovascular workout with ballet, jazz, modern, tap, African, hip—hop and other styles incorporated. This will give the dancers a feel of a real master class and get them in shape so that their technique and endurance are built. Also, the leader has the dancers move across the floor executing transitional movements such as walking, running, skipping, leaping, turning, gymnastics, kicks, jumps, hops, etc.

Dance Combinations—Now it is time for the dancers to learn some of the dance combinations to the upcoming dance. Depending on the time frame, the leader can teach the dancers a section of the dance, have dance captains to break the dancers in groups and go over troubled spots and then instruct the dancers to come back to put the steps together. Usually, if the class is structured as above, the leader can go over two to three dances a class. Our ministry ministers twice a month, so I work on those two dances and sometimes introduce the dance for the next month to them. The leader never wants his or her dancers to try to learn something at the last minute.

If we have future outside ministry engagements, they will work on those routines as well.

Announcements—The best time to make upcoming announcements and reminders is at the end of the class before the closing prayer. Some dancers have a habit of coming late and parents say that they did not know about something they were supposed to act upon. This way, the parents are there to pick up the children and are able to hear everything. Everyone is focused and ready to go, so the leader has their attention. Also, the leader can pass out any handouts that the children might forget to give to their parents. The leader can pass out the handouts to the parents and members to ensure they have received the information.

Closing Prayer—During this prayer, the leader can have dancers state their prayer requests and praise reports if they were late and missed the beginning of class.

Choreography Formations/Stage Directions

An effective dance should use the entire space of the sanctuary. Dancers should sometimes be able to dance in the pulpit area, on the steps, in front of the communion table, in front of the pews, down the aisles, in the balcony and in the back. There are blind spots in every church, so dancers should be everywhere so that everyone is being ministered.

A good choreographer will understand stage directions and formations. They will know *downstage, upstage, stage right and stage left.* They will let the dancers enter or exit out of every door of the sanctuary for a dramatic effect. All of these directions will not happen during one dance but in different dances to keep the congregation surprised. Also, they will know how to move the dancers in different formations during the dance such as *a straight line, two lines or several lines, a circle, a box, a diagonal, triangles, semi circles, a cross, etc.* Below are diagrams of some of the formations mentioned:

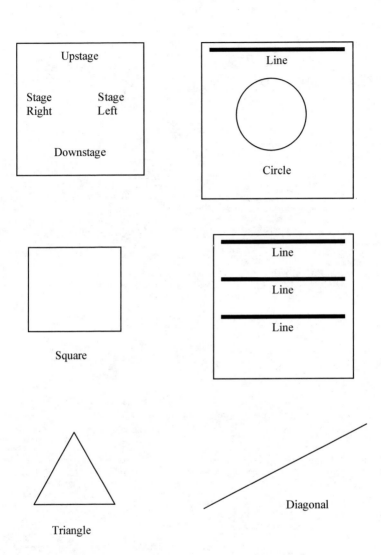

Upstage

Stage Right   Stage Left

Downstage

Line

Circle

Square

Line

Line

Line

Triangle

Diagonal

4

There are several steps to preparing for a worship service. Some leaders, pastors or lay people think that they can just request for a dance ministry to dance and that is it. It entails so much more that it usually takes a good two weeks to a month to prepare, especially if the ministry only meets once a week. Therefore, the ministry only has four rehearsals to prepare. The leader has to know what is the sermon or theme, which scriptures to prepare, if a narration should be prepared, which colors and praise garments to prepare, what is the stage layout for that day (i.e. will there be mikes, cords, speakers or will the pulpit be moved), how many dressing rooms are needed, which part of the service will the dance take place, etc.

The leader should pray at the beginning of the assignment and ask God which message and how He wants it to be conveyed. The Holy Spirit will let the leader know which song to use, what chore-ography to use, what colors or praise garments to incorporate, which formations to use, if He wants a narration, which style of dance and how He wants the congregation to be involved.

The night before, there should be a universal fast from every member of the ministry to see what direction God wants the dance to minister and if He wants any changes to occur. He might want to use the dancers prophetically. The fast is also a time for the dancers to ask God to bless the dance and ministry. A good time frame for the fast could be from 6:00 p.m. until 6:00 a.m. since there are a lot of baby Christians in the ministry. The dancers have to be taught discipline gradually.

The dancers should arrive at church an hour before the service begins. During this time, they will pray at the altar while the leader anoints them with oil; practice in the space; change into their clothes; fix make—up and hair; pray a blessing over the ministry; go into small areas of the dressing room and meditate individually to get in a ministering frame of mind; and get into their places for the dance five minutes before their entrance.

Once the dancers minister, they can go back to the dressing room to change clothes and then go into the sanctuary to participate during the remaining part of the service as a group in a reserved section. After service they can leave if it is one service. If the church has two services, the dancers can go back to the dressing rooms for snacks and then go to their Sunday school classes. They will meet back into the dressing rooms at least 30 minutes before the next service to start the process all over again.

Selecting Appropriate Praise Garments/Colors

Some dance ministries do not fully understand this area. They try to find something quick and affordable that all of the dancers can wear. Sometimes, they use examples from secular dance groups such as the leotard, a form fitting skirt or pants, tight leggings, t—shirts, black pants, etc. They wear the same outfit for all of the dances and usually, dance barefoot not wanting to invest in dance shoes. They use the word *costume* instead of what the Bible uses, *praise garment*.

This is why the leader has to be an anointed, Bible studying and prophetic person. They will be able hear from God and use only what the Bible used in biblical times. David and the high priests wore ephods, robes, tunics, sashes, headbands, a breastpiece and undergarments that were beautifully and exquisitely made for worship by skilled craftsmen. These pieces had onyx stones, jewels and the names of their tribe. The sashes, headbands and tunics meant dignity and honor. Below are the praise garments or priestly garments described in Exodus 28 and 29:

Ephod—This is the most important item of the priestly garments. It looked like an apron, which was made of materials woven out of gold and linen thread. It was made of gold, blue, purple and scarlet yarn and twisted linen. It covered the back and chest, and it reached nearly to the knees. It fastened to the body by two straps and a waistband. It, also, had two shoulder pieces attached to two of its corners, so it could be fastened.

The Breastpiece—It was made similar to the ephod with gold, blue, purple and scarlet yarn and twisted linen. It was made square— a span long and a span wide and folded double. It had four rows of precious stones mounted on it. It had two braided gold rings for it to fasten at the two corners of the breastpiece. Two more gold rings were attached to the other two corners of the breastpiece on the inside and two more rings to attach the bottom of the shoulder pieces on the front of the ephod. As a memorial to the Lord, the names of the sons of Israel were engraved over the heart. This was on Aaron's breast piece, and he wore it every time he entered the Holy Place.

Robe—It was entirely blue with an opening for the head in its center. It had a woven edge like a collar around the opening so that it did not tear. The hem was trimmed in blue, purple and scarlet yarn with gold bells between them. The sound of the bells was heard as Aaron entered in to the Holy Place before the Lord and when he came out. This allowed him not to die because only the high priests could enter into the Holy Place.

Tunics/Sashes/Turbans/Headbands/Undergarments—A blue cord was fastened to the front of the turban. This was worn on Aaron's forehead as a reminder of the guilt involved in the sacred gifts the Israelites had consecrated so they will be acceptable to the

Lord. These garments were made of fine linen and represented dignity and honor.

Before the priests wore these garments, they were consecrated. Today, dance ministries might not be so extreme, but they do follow some of the same principles and make their garments beautiful and extraordinary. They dress loosely covering up all parts of the body. The Feast Dress pattern is a garment that looks good on most size dancers. Instead of them wearing leggings, they wear culottes (wide leg pants) underneath their dresses. Silk Essence is a lightweight fabric that comes in beautiful colors, is easy to laundry and travels well. Most men wear tunics, ephods, vests or regular shirts and pants:

> Bless the Lord, O my soul. O Lord my God, thou art very great; thou art clothed with honour and majesty. Who coverest thyself with light as with a garment: who stretchest out the heavens like a curtain:[1] ("Psalms 104:1–2")

> Awake, awake; put on thy strength, O Zion; put on thy beautiful garments, O Jerusalem, the holy city: for henceforth there shall no more come into thee the uncircumcised and the unclean.[2] ("Isaiah 52:1")

> I will greatly rejoice in the Lord, my soul shall be joyful in my God; for he hath clothed me with the garments of salvation, he hath covered me with the robe of righteousness, as a bridegroom decketh himself with ornaments, and as a bride adorneth herself with her jewels.[3] ("Isaiah 61:10")

Colors—In the Bible, certain colors meant certain things or symbols. It is really awesome when a dance ministry incorporates colors into their theme or dance. Remember, a dance has the same results as a sermon—it wins souls. The closer the dance is to the scripture, the better the congregation can visualize and understand what God was saying in the text. A narration can be used before the dance to explain the colors and scriptures of the dance. This will really minister to the people, and they will be more aware of what the dance means. God, usually, relates to symbols, numbers and colors. All have significant meanings, and He usually speaks through each clearly. Below are some colors and their meanings:

COLOR	MEANING	SCRIPTURES
White	purity, cover nakedness, righteousness, light, holy, salvation, bride's garments	Dan. 7:9, 12:10; Eccl. 9:8; Rev. 3:5, 7:9, 19:8
Blue	heavenlies, Holy Spirit, God's commandments	Ex. 24:10; Num. 15:38; Ezek. 1:26
Gold	divinity, refinement, divine nature	Ex. 37, 40:5 & 26; Rev. 3:18; Ez 1:4, 8:2
Purple	royalty, majesty, kingship	Judges 8:26; Mark 15:17-18; John 19:2
Red	blood, atonement, sacrifice, redemption, forgiveness	Lev. 14:52, Josh. 2:18 & 21; Isaiah 1:18; Mat. 27:28; Heb 9:22
Yellow	God's glory, celebration, unclean	Lev. 13:30-36; Ezek. 1:4-8:2
Green	life everlasting, prosperity, freshness	Psalms 37:35, 52:7-8, 92:12-14; I John 5:10-14
Iridescent	overcoming, precious stones	Rev. 4:3, 21:11
Silver	redemption	Mat. 27:3-9
Orange	praise	I Chron. 23:13
Red/Orange/Yellow	fire, Holy Spirit, praise & worship, consuming fire	Acts 2:3; Lev. 3:3; Mal. 3:2; Heb. 13:15
Rainbow	God's promises, covenant	Gen. 9:13 & 16; Rev 4:3
Black	sin, death, calamity, famine, mourning, evil, humiliation	Psalms 23:4; Lam. 4:8-5:10; John 3:19-20; Eph. 5:9-13
Bronze/Brass	judgment	Micah 4:13; Rev. 2:18

Worship Service Format/Placement of the Dance

The worship service should be viewed as the Worship Experience. Too often, believers take church for granted and subconsciously view it as a job or something out of obligation. When this occurs, it becomes impossible for the Holy Spirit to have full reign because the congregation will expect tradition and think that anything else added to the service is unnecessary, emotional and intrusive.

As dance ministries are becoming rampant across the country, it is very important that they are integrated into the church service in an excellent way bringing full glory to God. Most universal churches have an "Order of Worship" or a programming format that they follow to make sure that the service runs smoothly. A proposed "Order of Worship" is as follows:[4]

Prelude—This occurs at the beginning of the service as a time of meditation, reflection and preparation in silent prayer. It is, usually, accompanied by soft, instrumental music.

Suggested Incorporated Dance Movements: A small group of dancers may fill the front or pulpit area by doing movements of reverence. The positions may be prostration, prayer or welcoming the presence of God individually or collectively.

Invocation—The opening corporate prayer of the service in which the Holy Spirit is welcomed to rule in authority over the service and participants.

Suggested Incorporated Dance Movements: It can be done either to music that invites the presence of the Holy Spirit specifically with matching movements or be a combination of spoken prayer by the minister or laity while the dance minister interprets the prayer through movement.

Procession—Ceremonial movement that occurs at the beginning of a service to a hymn or musical selection. The clergy, choir, dancers, elders, spiritual officers and all participants of the service move or march to their places. Procession symbolizes the gathering of God's people in preparation for the worship service.

Suggested Incorporated Dance Movements: Since procession is a symbol of triumph, the dancers can come down the aisles in a single file or in all of the aisles in unified order carrying candles, Bibles, streamers, banners, batons or with nothing at all.

Praise and Worship—This time is set aside for the psalmist, choir, musicians and dancers to lead the congregation into the presence of the Lord. This time is setting the atmosphere for the people to receive the Word of God. They are praising God for what He has done and worshipping Him for who He is.

Suggested Incorporated Dance Movements: A powerful way to engage the whole church is through the use of congregational dance. These movements are expressive, easy and repetitive so that the young and old can praise the Lord corporately. Sign language can also be used during this time, especially if the congregation has some deaf people visiting the church or if they are members.

Scripture Reading—This is the time when the Word of God is read aloud or sang corporately. The selected biblical text correlates with the sermon to be delivered.

Suggested Incorporated Dance Movements: Only the dance minister who knows the Word of God thoroughly and has an extensive movement vocabulary should interpret the reading of the scripture. He or she should be able to change movement thoughts at short notice while maintaining the anointing. The movements should be done with clarity, power and authority.

Main Selection—This could be done with a soloist or the entire dance team to instrumental, spoken word or to music with lyrics. It can also be ministered through dramatic interpretation. Any style of dance can be used as long as it is inspiring, comforting and encouraging God's people.

Suggested Incorporated Dance Movements: This part of the service can be altered between the choir, soloists, dancers, dramatists and mimes. Sometimes, it could be a combined effort between these ministries. The movements and music could be fast or slow, props can be incorporated and different colors or praise garments can be used to make the words come to life.

Tithes and Offering—This is the opportunity where the congregation can be given the opportunity to give monetarily as a cheerful giver.

Suggested Incorporated Dance Movements: If the congregation is being served in their seats, then the dancers can minister a lively piece that engages them in the dance as well. If the congregation has been directed to bring their money to the front of the church, the pastor or worship leader can encourage them to dance forward with their offering as a true "sacrifice of praise".

Sermon—This is the pivotal point in the worship service where the minister proclaims the Good News of Jesus Christ through the preaching and teaching of the Word.

Suggested Incorporated Dance Movements: A sermon can be preached, taught or danced powerfully through the creative innovation of the Holy Spirit. A team of dancers can build a sermon though the combined usage of the spoken word and dance interpretation, based on a pre—selected scriptural text. This should be done by dance ministers who have been called to the preaching ministry.

Invitation to Christian Discipleship or Altar Call—This is the time that lost souls are given the opportunity to give their lives to Jesus Christ. The altar call is an opportunity for believers to repent, receive forgiveness and deliverance.

Suggested Incorporated Dance Movements: This dance must be evangelistic in nature. It can be done before, during or after the initial invitation to salvation. The dance should seal the message of the preached word and have the anointing to save souls.

Benediction—This is the closing prayer and blessing given by the minister over God's people. This can be declarative or prophetic. It seals and confirms all that had occurred during the service.

Suggested Incorporated Dance Movements: Just as the opening prayer of the service, this dance can be a combination of spoken prayer and music.

Recessional—This is the end of the service in which the clergy, choir and worship participants formally exit from the service.

Suggested Incorporated Dance Movements: Congregational dance can be executed again while everyone is singing and exiting.

Getting the Church to Understand
Dance Ministry

Stated above is the ideal way that dance can be executed during the worship service. Getting the church to understand that is a challenge. If the church is traditional, it will probably except dance during the praise and worship, as the main selection or right before the sermon. If the church is more charismatic, it will probably allow the Holy Spirit to be creative and move during the service at different times as needed.

Again, the dance leader can meet with the pastor, church council, and minister of music to discuss the vision that God has for the dance ministry and church. The dance ministry vision needs to line up with the church's vision. The leader should always share scriptures that back up dance ministry and prepare narrations for the congregation before the dance presentations. This way everything will be clear on what God is trying to convey to the church through the dance.

Entertainment vs. Ministry

Once the dance leader has met with the pastor and church leaders, prepared narrations, and has allowed the Holy Spirit to operate sometimes in each section of the service as described above, the dance ministry will not be viewed as entertainment anymore. The church will see that it is a ministry. The key is to get the congregation involved, especially during praise and worship with congregational dance. If the congregation is busy praising God dancing during that time, they will not have time to stop and watch the dancers. The congregation will only do what the pastor or leadership instructs. Direction has to start from the top and trickle down to the congregation.

The congregation might be a little reluctant if they see a dance during the prayer, scripture, processional, benediction or as the main sermon. Once it gets instilled in the members and they see the spirit move, dance will become a natural part of the service. Like everything else, the congregation and leadership have to be trained.

Also, if the dance ministry is asked to minister at another church or another event, the dance leader has to train that representative as well. One time another church asked for my dancers to participate in its Youth Explosion. I asked the leader what type of dance or which group. I could tell that she did not understand and got a little short with me and kept saying, "Praise Dancers." I knew in my spirit that churches use that term lightly and refer to most teams as "Praise Dancers." Listening to her describe the event, I knew that she did not want "Praise Dancers." Praise dancers only do light repetitive movements for the congregation to join. She did not want repetitive movements, she wanted a performance. I explained to her that we do all types of dance such as ballet, jazz, tap, African, hip—hop, banners, flags, warfare, drama, pantomime, prophetic, etc. I had to train her to understand what she really wanted and not to put all liturgical dance groups in the same category as "Praise Dancers" because that is exactly what she would get, "Praise Movements." That is why we call our dancers at church a dance ministry because we minister unto the Lord and His people using different facets of dance, drama, arts, spoken word, props, etc.

Paid vs. Nonpaid

This issue varies among different churches and ministries. Most churches do not pay their dance ministry leader or dancers because they feel if they are a member of the church, that is their reasonable service. They feel that the ministry is tithing their time unto God. The churches also feel that if they pay one ministry, they have to pay for another one. They still do not fully understand what dance ministry entails, and that is very expensive to buy praise garments, make props, etc. Usually, it takes long and extra rehearsals prior to an event or worship service. If children are in the ministry, the leader usually has to use his or her vehicle to pick up children sometimes, stay late when parents come late, put his or her own money in the ministry, do administrative work, call people about last minute changes, etc.

Some churches put their minister of dance and minister of music on staff. They realize that they have to pay musicians, guest preachers, singers or dancers, and anyone else coming to the church to minister. The pastor knows that when he or she goes to other churches, he or she will usually get paid or receive a love offering. He or she realizes that the dance minister is a minister just like the musicians and other preachers. They will honor them if the dance minister is an ordained minister or has a Master's or Doctor of Ministry degree:

> A man's gift maketh room for him, and bringeth him before great men.[5] ("Proverbs 18:16")

It is up to the individual pastor or church if either of them feel led by the Holy Spirit or if can afford to pay a dance minister. The dance minister should not expect pay or only do the ministry for the money even if he or she does get paid. This is God's work, and it is our reasonable service to honor and praise Him with our gifts.

Flowing Together with the Pastor/Music Leader

In order for the worship service to run smoothly, the dance minister, pastor and minister of music need to be on one accord. They need to all understand the vision the Lord has for the church and try not to upstage the other. It is God's service, and the Holy Spirit will run the service as He wills.

Usually, the dancers, praise team and musicians minister together during praise and worship. When the church is led into worship, the Holy Spirit might have one dancer to lead or one singer. The pastor, dance leader and minister of music should have certain eye or hand signals so that it will be known when one of them needs to minister, sit down, have someone in their group or whole team to minister, if it a time for prayer or for the whole congregation to dance.

Evangelism

Once the dance ministry has been established at church, God will send the ministry out to minister to the unsaved and at other Christian events. We were created to praise and worship God. The Bible did not say that we are to only praise Him in the privacy of our homes or at church. We are to witness about His goodness wherever we go and we do not have to necessarily do it verbally. We can dance the story of salvation. Sometimes, our life can just be a witness. People are always watching Christians to see how they are living. Jesus commanded us to witness in all nations:

> Go ye therefore, and teach all nations, baptizing them in the name of the Father, and of the Son, and of the Holy Ghost: Teaching them to observe all things whatsoever I have commanded you: and, lo, I am with you alway, even unto the end of the world.[6] ("Matthew 28:19–20")

This type of witnessing is called evangelism. Evangelism is the act of announcing the salvation news to others and leading them to the grace and mercy of God. In these last days, He is going to move us quickly to places that are not usually ministered to by His people. We need to be the Ark of the Covenant so that people will look at us and see that we have something they need. He is going to move us in new or controversial areas such as dance in the church and as a way to reach the lost. He will not only use anyone who will go to where He wants, but also He will use the "nobody's." The "nobody's" in the Bible became great in God because they trusted in Him and not in their flesh. God received all of the glory when He used the "nobody's" because they were not naturally capable of doing what He did through them. People always say, "God, I will go where you want me to go. Do what you want me to do and say what you want me to say." Do they really mean that? When it boils down to it, people think inside of the box, but God thinks on the outside of the box. Below are some opportunities that God can use His people to evangelize to lost souls:

A. *Outreaches*
   1. Productions
      a. Seasonal and Non—Seasonal
         1. In Churches
            a. Illustrated Sermons
            b. Seminars and Workshops
         2. For Schools
         3. TV

   2. Festivals of Praise
      a. Concert Setting
      b. Celebration

   3. Community
      a. Park Meetings
      b. Prison Ministry
      c. Convalescent Home Ministry
      d. Shopping Malls and Swap Meets
      e. Parades
      f. Weddings
      g. Reunions
      h. Baby Showers
      i. Birthday Parties

B. *Reaching The Nations*
   1. Dance teams can sometimes go where pastors and ministers cannot

   2. Dancers will draw crowds
      a. Tambourines draw people with their sound
      b. Flags and banners catch people's attention with their eyes

   3. Ethnic dances and costumes will attract attention

Dance can be used even more as a powerful outreach tool that will draw attention and save souls. God will use any vehicle that is dramatic, colorful and creative to hold the attention of the lost. He knows that people love to be entertained in the secular world, so that is why He uses dance in the Christian world for salvation.

5

Some dance ministries prepare an in—house concert for their church and the local community. We minister in concert every June to exhibit the different styles of dance and the ways a dance ministry can praise the Lord. Usually, during a worship service we have to be careful what we wear or what style of music to use. During a concert, we can be more liberal with styles and colors. This will not even offend most people because it is in a different setting. My group probably would not minister a hip—hop style dance during the worship service, but would do one during the concert. It would offend someone because he or she would relate it to secular. God does not care about which style a ministry uses as long as it brings glory to His name. That is why during the concert we educate the audience with narrations, so they will understand through scripture the meanings of the words, music and movements.

There are so many facets to putting together a concert for a church. It is still similar to a secular Broadway production. An effective concert has to have a budget, bulletin announcements, facility requests/meetings, advertisements, flyers, invitations, invitations to participating churches, selection of songs and theme, a rehearsal schedule, costumes (praise garments), costume/praise garment committee, uniformed hairstyles, props/prop design, stage director, stage assistants, parent assistants, stage directions, narrations, programs, permission licenses, photographer, videographer, gifts/tokens of appreciation for volunteers, etc.

Budget—Before rehearsals begin, a budget has to be established. A concert can be very costly and sometimes the church might assist with some of the costs, and sometimes the leader or dancers might have to come up with some of the costs. The budget will be itemized by some of the items mentioned above. It is good to treat everything as a business and have invoices or quotes attached to the check requests. If the leader pays for some of the items, he or she might pay up front for some things and then the church might reimburse him or her later. It is good to write the concert expenses into the general annual dance ministry budget at the beginning of the year. An estimated cost for a concert is around $4000.00. Other options for the ministry to afford the concert would be through fundraising or sponsorships (See Appendix Example #23).

Bulletin Announcement—The ministry should start advertising the need for assistants for the concert in the church bulletin, video screens, bulletin e—letter or pulpit about two months before the event. The initial announcement will ask for volunteers in every area of the concert such as stage assistants, costume seamstresses, prop/stage designers, people with computer skills, public speakers, actors, dancers, etc. The announcements that are made closer to the concert should only be to promote the event and encourage people to attend (See Appendix Example #24).

Facility Requests/Meetings—In order to have a successful concert, the leader has to meet with the different department heads at the church to make sure that everything will run smoothly and so that they will know everything the ministry needs financially and operationally. For any ministry to use any room, hallway, dressing room or set—up a room, the leader has to fill out a facility request and get it approved. They have to make sure that another ministry is not requesting the same room or service at the same time on the same date. Also, the leader makes requests for media services, lighting, rehearsal time, fundraisers, food or usage of church supplies and services (See Appendix Example #25).

Advertisements—Most churches will arrange for the concert to be announced as a PSA on most radio and television stations. It will also be mentioned in the local newspaper under events. Since our church is a well—known church and tries to involve the whole community, we will purchase advertisements on the radio, television, cable, etc. We not only use the concert as an evangelistic opportunity but also as a teaching tool for other ministries on how to run properly an effective dance ministry.

Advertising will be one of the most expensive items in the budget. It could easily run between $1000.00–$2000.00. Every once in a while, the station will work out a really nice package deal with the church.

Flyers—For any concert or production, flyers need to be distributed everywhere, so people will know about the event. They can go on the cars, be given out after church in the lobby and parking lot, mailed out to churches and put at the cash register at some retail stores or bookstores.

Invitations—Invitations need to be sent out to churches, pastors, schools, colleges, other dance ministries and who ever personally the leader wants to attend. Since the concert is a learning tool for dance ministries, the leader tries to reach out to any similar ministry with children, youth and adults. The invitations can be printed out professionally or printed on some pretty paper. This depends on the budget of the ministry (See Appendix Example #26).

Invitations to Participating Churches—Some concerts only feature the dance ministry hosting the concert, or they can feature other solo artists and dance ministries. If the leader decides to invite another dance ministry, they need to send a formal letter of invitation to the pastor or dance leader of the invited church (See Appendix Example #27).

Selection of Songs and Theme—The leader should fast, pray and seek God to which songs to use and what theme He wants to convey to His people. Our concert themes usually start off with a prayer or prophetic dance, then move to praise, worship, thanksgiving, attacks of the enemy, testimonies of His Goodness, forgiveness, salvation and victory. The theme follows a Christian's walk through salvation. The songs and dances have to show that along with the narrations and scriptures.

Since our ministry displays different styles of dance, our songs have to lend themselves to those styles. It, also, has to be a mixture of slow and fast songs and songs that relate to the young and old.

Rehearsal Schedule—The ministry should start rehearsing at least two months before the concert. They can use some of the dances that they ministered during the year. These dances will be only a review. If other ministries or guest dancers are involved, the leader can start rehearsing with them about 3 weeks before the concert. About 3 songs should be worked on during each rehearsal adding a new song a week. There might be an extra rehearsal during the week added the closer it gets to the concert. It is good for the leader to come up with a printed schedule for the dancers and parents to have (See Appendix Example #28).

Costumes/Praise Garments—In sacred or religious dance, costumes are called praise garments or priestly garments. The leader should pray and ask God what type of garments to wear and what colors does He want to minister through to His people. Some dance ministries use a general praise garment for everything. This might be due to the lack of finances. For a dance, message or scripture to come alive, the praise garments need to be exactly as the scripture described. Each scene should be different, colorful and appropriate for the theme. Every dancer should be fully covered not leaving any room for their skin to show too much through the fabric.

If the theme is praise, the dancers can wear praise robes or ephods; if the theme is about angels or demons, they need to wear wings, halos or black with messy make—up; if the theme is about the "Blood of Jesus" or "Forgiveness," they need to wear red; and if a dancer is playing Jesus, he or she needs to wear a white robe with silver meaning redemption.

Costume/Praise Garment Committee—These are parents or people who can sew or create praise garments, banners, flags or props. They are very artistic, creative and can also draw, paste, cut, or laminate signs very well. They work closely with the director/ choreographer in trying to bring to life the vision the Lord gave the leader. If they are anointed, they can listen to the music or read the related scripture and come up with really awesome works and designs.

Uniformed Hairstyles—Most dance ministries are majority of women and girls. In order to minister in an undistracting way, the dancers should always pull their hair back in a bun unless the dance calls for freestyle hair movements or if the hair is part of the chore-ography. If a female dancer is playing a demon, she might wear her hair wild and teased. Just like in secular dances, dancers wear their hair pulled back. This is common in formal ballet classes. Ministers of dance should use the same concept in church. They are there to minister and be on one accord. God wants excellence and order in church. Also, dancers should not wear earrings when they are ministering unless that is part of the praise garment. Since everyone does not have pierced ears and clip on earrings would fall off during the dance, earrings should not be worn so that everyone will be on one accord.

Props/Prop Design—The same principle goes for props and prop design. The props should not overshadow the dance, only enhance it. Props can be small enough for the hands or as big as a set in a play. It depends on what God wants for each scene. For a church concert, one backdrop, banner or set can be used for the entire time. If this concept is used, then small props, chairs, a tap board, hats, gloves, pantomime make—up, crosses, tombs, or palm leaves can be used. The dancers have to be able to concentrate and dance well while holding or maneuvering a prop so that they will not drop it.

Stage Director—This is one of the most important roles for the concert. This person oversees all of the stage assistants and works closely with the director/choreographer. They organize the roles of the stage assistants. They know every scene, the order of the concert, which scenes need props, where each dressing room is located, which dancers are in certain dressing rooms, and all of the logistics of the concert.

Stage Assistants—These people help with setting up the stage design, placing or removing props, queuing the dancers, organizing the props, collecting them and returning them in order to the prop room, etc. The timing of the scenes and between the scenes has to run quickly and smoothly. These people have to practice that over and over to make that happen. If a two—hour concert has 30 to 50 people involved, there needs to be about 10–20 stage assistants. This works well if the concert has around 10–15 scenes.

Parent Assistants—This is another key role especially if children are involved in the concert. The parents help with pinning praise garments, combing hair, organizing the dressing rooms, assigning dancers to parents for dressing assistance, assigning and collecting of small hand props, applying pantomime make—up and other duties as assigned.

Stage Directions—Once the theme, scenes, props, praise garments, solos and characters have been set, there needs to be a formal stage direction diagram or format for the sound, lighting, videographer, stage director, stage assistants, parent assistants and dancers to follow. This format should contain the name of each dance, the dancers assigned to each dance, which praise garments are in each dance, which stage props are used, and what the screens should display during the dances (See Appendix Example #29).

Narrations—To enhance each dance and for the audience to get the full understanding of the story and related scripture, narrations need to be prepared. Usually the director or choreographer writes them unless the Holy Spirit inspires another member of the team. This is because the choreographer or director knows what the choreography means and why he or she arranged the dance the way he or she did. He or she has usually prayed and sought God on the scriptures and message. Usually, each dance has a narration. Our concert last year had one narration per two songs to save time. Our previous concerts were extremely long when we added the narrations, so we cut down the time by using this concept. When writing a narration, a leader should make sure that they are sermonettes. They should tell the related scripture, how it relates to the dance and how it relates to the people now in their daily walk with Christ (See Appendix Example #30).

Programs—The programs need to be sent to a professional printer. Depending on what style, size, the logo, how much color is used and the quantity, the price can vary. The average cost for us to get 500–1000 printed was between $500.00–$750.00. The programs should have the bios of the director/choreographer and stage director; the order of dances; the ministry participants, guest dancers, guest ministries; and acknowledgements (See Appendix Example #31).

Permission/Licenses—This is a topic that most churches or dance ministries do not know a lot about or understand. Dance is just like the music industry. It is a part of the music industry. There has to be permission to use someone's music, ideas, choreography or to sell audio or videotapes. A church or individual can be sued if another company's, choreographer's or writer's material is used.

A choreographer should always get his or her dances copyrighted by the Library of Congress. When other dancers or choreographers see really good ideas they might use those same ideas for their groups. They do not know that it is a crime because people have been making copies of CD's, carbon copies of documents and movies for years. It is not expensive to get choreography copyrighted. It is $45.00 per song or series. It still costs the same price if there are several songs on one tape such as a concert. If a dance group has an annual concert, it can copyright all of them as a series for one price. The videotapes should have the copyright symbol, year and the person who had it copyrighted. A copyright example would be: Copyright © 2004 by John Doe.

If a choreographer wants to dance to a song, he or she needs to get permission from the writer or publishing company. The writer or publishing company probably will not mind if the choreographer is using the dance for a worship service, and the church decides to sell the tapes. This is because most churches have a blanket permission license from Christian Copyright Licensing International (CCLI). They still to check to see if all of the songwriters or publishers on the tape are members of CCLI. If they are not, they are probably a member of American Society of Composers, Authors and Publishers (ASCAP) or Broadcast Music, Inc. (BMI). The choreographer can find this information on the CD jacket next to the song or they can go on—line to see if the writer or publisher is a member at either www.ascap.com or www.bmi.com.

If the churches are going to sell the videotapes from their annual concert, they will have to get permission and purchase a license from these companies so that the companies can make a percentage off of every sell. A dance concert is not covered or protected under the worship service blanket permission license. Also, the choreographer gets a percentage of the sells because it is their original work. One license can cost between $300 to $600. The choreographer or church might be able to negotiate with ASCAP or BMI to pay for an annual license if they are going to use that dance or dances more than once. An individual dancer can also negotiate an annual fee if he or she is going to minister that dance at different places such as reunions, weddings, graduations, etc. These companies might not charge anything as long as tapes are not being sold. It is good just to let those organizations know so they will be aware of the church's intentions.

A choreographer or church might have to purchase several licenses for one song. He or she can either purchase a song and dance license, synchronization license or a license from the actual recording studio where the CD was mixed. It depends if the dance is done live, on TV, synchronized with music or if the music or words are altered for the dance or concert. Sometimes, if the company has a blanket license, the choreographer might have to be required to get one. When our group was on The Bobby Jones Show, we still had to get permission from the writer of the song we used even though this TV show had a blanket license. When we were on Trinity Broadcasting Network (TBN), we did not have to get a license. It is up to the company. The church should have their attorney research these requirements.

Dance studio teachers are required to purchase an annual license just to play music in their studios or during their recitals. From time to time, ASCAP or BMI will monitor studios to see what they are playing because they know that sometimes dancers will make copies of the CDs.

Photographer—Because of the different scenes, colors and praise garments, the director or choreographer will request to have a professional photographer. The general price for a photographer can range from $200–$300. The photographer will make additional money after the concert because when the parents and participants see how nice the pictures look; they will buy additional ones for their family and friends. The photographer will either make a nice photo album for the group or put the pictures on a CD and e–mail them.

A good photography company will have several photographers covering the concert so that they can feature all of the dances, positions, scenes, fast movements, flips, close—ups and long shots. They also need to be stationed in the balcony, in the aisles, across the front, on the stage, in the pulpit, etc. They should not take away from the concert or distract the audience or videographer.

Videographer—The choreographer, church leaders, concert committee, media team and videographer should have pre—concert meetings to make sure that everyone is on one accord. They need to decide if the videotapes will be sold, if permission licenses should be purchased and what angles and shots are important to the choreographer. The videographer needs to come to the dress rehearsals so that they can get an idea of the concert format.

Once the concert is over, the videographer and choreographer need to meet to edit the tapes before they are viewed or sold. Most videographers have a team who will do live edits during the concert. Also, the videographer must put that the concert is copyrighted on the tapes if the choreographer got the choreography or concept copyrighted. The videotapes should not be sold until everything is copyrighted and the permission is cleared by the publishing companies.

Sound/Lighting Technician—This crew is responsible for cueing and playing the music and cueing up or down the lights. The crew needs to attend the planning meetings as well. The choreographer should give the crew and the videographer a stage direction script to follow. Also, the sound technician should make a general CD with all of the songs of the concert. This way he will not have to find or cue different CDs.

Screen Coordinator—Most churches have video screens all over the church so that everyone can see no matter where they sit. This coordinator should attend planning meetings and also have a script to follow. They should have a copy of the program so that they can display the correct spelling of names, songs, soloists and scenes. The screens should show close—ups of the dances so that people sitting far away can see very well.

Gifts/Tokens of Appreciation—Most church leaders do not give their volunteers individual gifts. They might give an annual retreat or dinner. Sometimes, volunteers receive certificates. Since I have a secular dance teaching background, I choose to give individual gifts to people who assist with the production. It is protocol at the end of dance recitals for the teacher to give the students' gifts, certificates or trophies. This custom has been incorporated into our program at the church. Sometimes the gifts are purchased from the concert budget, or I will buy the gifts personally. It gets expensive, but I plan every year to buy gifts for all of the dancers, seamstresses, stage assistants, parent assistants, guest dancers, etc. These volunteers do excellent professional work that deserve great appreciation.

Reception (Optional)—It is nice if the church sponsors a light reception for the participants and their family members after the concert. If the budget allows, the reception can be extended to even the audience if they decide to stay. This gives the audience a chance to greet the participants in the concert and give their congratulations.

6

As the ministry grows, the leader needs to expose constantly the ministry to new ideas, master classes, other ministries, teachers, pastors, workout facilities and opportunities that will take its anointing to another level. The best time to explore these opportunities would be in the summer because the children are out of school and a lot of church members take vacations. Church attendance is sometimes low, and the ministry might not be asked to minister as much. The children do not have to focus on schoolwork or trying to get to their numerous after school practices and rehearsals. The adult members workload is lighter in the summer also.

This would be a good time for the ministry to have a year—end retreat, sabbatical or attend some conferences. At our church, I, purposely, have the dance ministry minister between September and June. The concert is in June and they are on sabbatical for the rest of the summer. Let us look at some of the annual activities a dance ministry can participate.

Year End Retreat

This can be done in seminar form, as a trip, master class or at a rented facility or cabin where the members will spend the night or weekend. The focus of the retreat is for the ministry to have reflections from the past year, look at ways to make it better, explore ways of growth and visualize how God is going to take them to the next level. The retreat can be structured or unstructured. It can still have the dance class format with several activities added.

Our first retreat was simple. It was in the format of a class mixed with a program, Bible study, food, master class and trip. We selected two days in the summer in the Family Life Center at our church. One of the nights we spent the night with sleeping bags. The Family Life Center has a basketball court, a bowling alley, a game room, a crafts room, a racquetball court, a weight room, a TV room, a skating rink and a kitchen. I chose this facility because the majority of our dancers are children, and I wanted us to have fun as well as work on our technique, bond with each other and focus on our relationship with God.

Permission Form—Before the ministry participates in any church activity, permission forms need to be filled out by participants and parents. This is vitally important if the ministry is going out of town. The form needs to have contact information, emergency contact information, illnesses listed, insurance information, physician information and a section where the dance member and parent sign their name and date (See Appendix Example #32).

Retreat Agenda—Below is the agenda our ministry used when we had our retreat in the Family Life Center (See Appendix Example #33):

Friday, June 15, 2001–7:00 p.m.
Welcome

Introduction of Participants

Praise Reports/Prayer Requests

Prayer

Bible Study/Book Review

Meditation Time/Song

Introduction of Speaker

Speaker—Della Perkins/Director, Christ The Rock Metro Church Dance Ministry

Master Ballet Class—Della Perkins

Food

Presentations

View Video Tapes

Holy Ghost Party Dance

Games/Sports/Fellowship

Sleepover

Saturday, June 16, 2001

7:00 a.m.—Prayer of Thanksgiving

7:15 a.m.—Shower/Dress

8:15 a.m.—Light Continental Breakfast

9:00 a.m.—Clean Up Family Life Center

9:30 a.m.—Leave for Casey Jones Village Restaurant—Jackson, TN

3:30 p.m.—Leave for Memphis, TN

4:40 p.m.—Return to Memphis, TN

This is just a sample of what a ministry can do during a retreat. Another time, our ministry rented out Bogey's Putt Putt and Family Entertainment Complex. We started out with the same Bible study, reflections, and speaker format. Then we served food; let everyone play video arcade games, golf, Putt Putt and ride the rides; rehearsed on our routines for the concert after the place closed; and slept over night.

A retreat is well needed for a large ministry that is constantly seeking God to go to another level. It can be spiritual and fun at the same time, so your ministry members can bond with each other and get closer to God.

Attending Conferences

Many liturgical dance praise and worship conferences are popping up across the world. Some are local, national or international. It is awesome to see the different cultures, denominations, colors, praise garments, banners, workshops, dance classes, worship services and dance ministries. Everyone might speak a different language, but they have one purpose to come and praise the Lord for hours with continuous music and dance.

It is good for leaders to attend a local conference and a national/international conference a year to keep abreast of the ever—changing world of liturgical dance. They can learn so much and bring a lot back to their church to take it to the next level. Also, they can build relationships with other dance ministry leaders and form a network of mentoring whenever they need advice, ideas, fellowship and ministry outreach opportunities.

Usually, a conference lasts from 3 days to a whole week. A typical format is breakfast, general worship service, workshops, lunch, workshops, rehearsals, and evening worship celebration (open to general public). Some of the classes are:

Tambourine Dancing

Hip—Hop

Flags

Banners

Streamers

Pantomime

Worship Dance

Congregational Dance

Sign Language

Israeli Dance

Multimedia in Worship

Special Effects

Embroidery Prayer

Choreography

Dance Ministry Leaders Class

Prophetic/Apostolic Dance

The Singing Congregation

Rebuilding the Tabernacle of David

Priestly Garments

Dances for Ministry

Drumming

African/Caribbean Dance

Creative Writing

Dance Ministry Protocol

Warfare

Billow Banners

Prophetic Drawing

Hearing the Call

Producing Celebrations

Modern Dance

Intercession within Movement and Dance

Worship Team Dynamics

Song Writing

Dancing Veils

Starting and Directing a Worship Dance Ministry

Leading Children in Worship Dance

Lyrical Dance

Redeeming the Arts in Worship

Drama

Purchasing Rehearsal Space

Sometimes, it is good for the leader to attend conferences alone so he or she can focus on everything. He or she should not miss a single thing, event or networking opportunity. If they bring their ministry, they are going to be focused on making sure that the chaperones are doing what they are supposed to do, if the children are following the rules, and if everyone is getting to where they need to go on time. When the whole ministry goes to a conference together, they begin to see the whole picture of dance ministry and what other ministries are doing. They finally realize the purpose of dance ministry and just not what their leader has said.

Initial Meeting/Agenda—Once the conference has been chosen, there should be an initial meeting to discuss it in general. The parents, dancers and potential chaperones should be in attendance. This meeting should be formal with an agenda (See Appendix Example #34). A suggested agenda should consist of prayer, general conference information, workshop information, registration and hotel information, conference and roommate sign—up information, fundraising activities, sponsorship ideas, testimony from a member who has attended a conference, video review of excerpts from the previous conference and closing prayer.

The Sign—Up Sheet—The leader should have a sign—up sheet to see who is interested in attending the conference. It does not have to be fancy. It needs to have the name, the chaperone's name, a checked mark in the participant, volunteer or registered box and a box for the members to mark if they are an adult or child (See Appendix Example #35.) Usually, the participants have to register on—line or through the mail. The amount of the conference is determined by the age, so it is very important for them to put their age range.

Fundraisers—Even if the church has a budget to send a ministry as large as a dance ministry with about 30 members, it is still good to fundraise to defray some of the costs. Depending on the time frame and commitment of the members, the fundraising activities should be able to assist everyone as a whole or as an individual. It, also, depends on if the ministry is flying on an airplane or traveling by bus. Some conferences have a registration fee between $75.00–$250.00. The ministry has to also consider hotel, spending money and if they want to purchase props, flags, music, banners or praise garments. A conference is always going to have vendors of every kind selling all kinds of dance ministry accessories. These items are usually very expensive. One flag can cost about $140.00 because the vendors make, paint and design them by hand and use high quality fabric. These flags are colorful, big and eye catching.

The ministry can engage in fundraisers such as car washes; Glamour You Pictures; selling candy, entertainment books, cookies, Krispy Kreme doughnuts/certificates, Pizza Hut certificates; bake sales; yard/garage sales; selling food at a professional basketball game in the concession stand; silent auctions; selling t—shirts and sun visors with the ministry logo; and selling jewelry and art. These are just to name a few but are great ways to make a lot of money in a little time.

If the church is really supportive, it might take up an offering during service after the ministry dances. This way the anointing is high and people are more receptive to give when they have truly been blessed. All the pastor has to do is announce that are representing the church and the congregation usually responds to the call.

Sponsorships—If the ministry does not want to fundraise or they have not made all of the money needed to attend the conference, it can solicit sponsors. Sponsors are individuals or companies that will pay for a certain event, activity or item for the trip. The leader should call or ask them in person if they would like to assist the ministry in attending the conference. If the individual or company agrees, the leader should send a sponsorship letter and proposal outlining in costs what the ministry would like for the sponsor to pay. The leader does not have to show all of the expenses, just the one he or she wants a particular sponsor to pay. The letter should remind the potential sponsor of their initial conversation, what they are asking, some history about the group or organization, the group's accomplishments and the attached proposal (See Appendix Example #36).

The proposal should be brief and to the point of what the ministry is asking. It should give exact figures and have the correct name and address of the company, so the sponsor can send the money directly to the company. When a sponsorship letter is sent out in corporate America, the person asking will offer benefits for the sponsor. Since this is ministry, the sponsor will not expect anything in return except his or her name mentioned. Sometimes, a very humble person does not want his or her name disclosed. He or she just wants to help the ministry.

If a sponsor does send money to assist the ministry, the leader should immediately send them a thank you letter. It does not have to be long, just specifically thanking him or her for what he or she donated (See Appendix Example #37). Even if the sponsor only gave a portion of what the leader asked, a thank you letter should still go forth.

Permission Letters for Participants—When the ministry has students in school and they have to be dismissed, the leader has to write a formal letter to the school system or college. They should attach the conference information or schedule to the letter for justification. The letter should be on the church's letterhead with the leader's signature.

The letter for the public or private school systems should state the purpose of the letter, what they are attending, where they are going, the date of the event, the requirements of the dancers, what they will be learning, the date of return, when they need to be dismissed, a check off of affected dates, the student's signature, the parent's signature, the principal's signature and the teacher's signature (See Appendix Example #38).

The letter for the college professors will basically state the same information. It will only have one check off box that shows the date(s) the student will be attending the conference.

Transportation Roster—All participants will receive a copy of the roster that indicates the ones who will be riding the bus, van or car. Since our ministry had some people who could not get off work or school early or had to come back early, we had some people riding the bus who stayed for the whole weekend. We also had the church van pick up the people who had to wait until 12:00 noon to get off work or school. They came a little later than the big bus and left a day earlier. We also had some people who preferred to drive their own car since they had to come later. This list will help the leader keep up with all of the different schedules just in case something happens or does not go as planned (See Appendix Example #39).

Hotel Room Assignments—Most conference hotels allow four people to share a room. If the hotel has suites in the agreement, then six people can share a room. Our ministry had this agreement, so we had six people to a room with one to two chaperones (See Appendix Example #40).

It is best for the ministry to stay at the host conference hotel because the services and workshops start early and end late. This way, people do not have to find a way back and forth to another hotel. Also, there is usually a discounted conference rate for participants.

Directions/Travel Itinerary—Once everything is established with the bus company, the leader needs to send formal directions on how the driver should get to the church from the bus company. If the ministry needs for the driver to take them extra places or to eat, it needs to be stated on this itinerary. This itinerary only needs to show the first and last day of travel (See Appendix Example #41).

This short section of the chapter showed an example of how a leader can organize his or her own group that is attending a conference. There are so many other different examples, but this works well if children are involved. With children, everything has to be more detailed. This information would be the same if the ministry is taking a big outreach trip, and they are going to minister instead of participate in a conference. Our ministry went to Toronto, Canada, and it took so much more to plan an international trip. There was so much more involved such as attaining passports, what one can take out or bring into the country, what types of dances and songs that would really minister to all types of cultures, denominations and beliefs, how to do an effective show without taking a lot of props, reducing costume/praise garment changes, etc.

A ministry is going to have to be prayerful on which direction God wants to lead them. They should be ready for many invitations after they have been exposed to the public. If they are really good, people and organizations will start asking them to minister. This outreach opportunity enlarges the ministry's territory.

Annual Sabbitical

An annual sabbatical is really needed for a ministry that is very physical and in great demand monthly. As mentioned in Ecclesiastes, it is a time for everything. It is a time to be busy and a time to rest and be still. Pastors take time for a sabbatical every year, so other ministries that are in the forefront need to learn to do the same thing as well.

If the leader does not say no, everyone will pull on the ministry and invite it to minister at church or at other engagements. Other churches or people who are over programs, weddings, reunions or graduations will ask the ministry to minister for these events. If they plan these events around holidays, it is not fair for the ministry to be available every time because some of the members may want to go out of town for that weekend. Even if most of the members are unavailable for that holiday, the leader has to change his or her personal plans and stay in town to oversee the dancer or dancers who is ministering. The ministry and leader will be burned out if they say yes to everything. They have to pray for wisdom on when to say yes and when to say no. Here are some reasons why dance ministries need to take a break, especially around the summer:

- Members and the leader need to rest so that their bodies can recuperate from all of the physical strain, activities and running around to rehearsals.
- The members need time to reflect on the year and on what ways they can improve as a member.
- The leader needs to reflect on how he or she can make the ministry more effective.
- The leader needs to hear from God on what direction He wants the ministry to move for the next year.
- The leader can plan and prepare for the upcoming auditions and re—assignment of officers.
- The leader can recover his or her bank account if he or she spent a lot of their personal money for props, materials or praise garments.
- The members and the leader can enjoy their personal life, family, friends and take vacations.
- The leader can attend conferences to learn new trends in dance ministry.
- The ministry can go on an outreach trip as a group or attend a conference.
- This time off gives other ministries a chance to be used during that time because it is not about one ministry being in the forefront all of the time.
- This gives children a break from schoolwork, remembering dance steps, after school practices and dance rehearsals. They need balance.
- This gives the congregation a chance not to get so dependant on one type of ministry.
- It builds anticipation on when the ministry is going to minister again.

Sabbaticals are a necessary part of the overall worship and arts ministry. The worship and arts ministry leader should have options and back—ups so when one ministry is taking a break, the services will still have a performing ministry available. This works well if the church has many different types of choirs. The Sanctuary Choir, Youth Choir, Children's Choir, Praise Team, Women's Chorus and the Men's Chorus can alternate between the different Sundays during the month. It is good even to invite a guest high school or touring Christian choir to minister.

The same plan can work if the church is large, and there are different dance teams. The praise dance team, the mime team, the children's team, the youth team, the adult team, the flag team, the sign language team or the prophetic team can alternate and dance on different Sundays.

Sabbaticals can work if planned appropriately. The leaders should pray and ask God how He wants to direct it. This way, everyone can still be blessed, and the service will not miss a beat.

Christian Dance Organizations

It is good for the ministry leader and even the members to belong to a professional dance organization. There are so many secular and Christian organizations to choose. It depends on what are the leader's strengths and interests. This information can be found on the Internet or at conferences. Just like in the professional realm, people from the same backgrounds, careers or interests can join these groups. Some of the groups in the secular world are National Black Journalists Association (NBJA), Toastmasters, Tennessee Association of Dance (TAD), Society of Human Resource Management (SHRM), etc.

Three Christian dance organizations that most dance ministry leaders should be a part of are the National Liturgical Dance Network (NLDN), Christian Dance Fellowship (CDF) and International Christian Dance Fellowship (ICDF).

The National Liturgical Dance Network (NLDN) is under the leadership of Minister Eyesha Marable. She is the Co—Director of the Greater New Allen AME Church in Jamaica, NY. This national organization is comprised of dance ministry leaders from around the country. They share ideas, assist each other with advice, conduct conferences, speak at churches and get together as a general ministry and minister a master dance at different functions. They also have a basic praise garment that members wear at different national functions, so they can be identified when they minister together. Some of the members purchase their praise garments from Minister Marable who has an Indian praise garment line of many different colors. The network members purchase the rainbow colored garment representing God's covenant with all of the represented groups.

The Christian Dance Fellowship (CDF) is under the leadership of Karla Jenkins of Dallas, TX and Pastor Pamela Rutherford Hardy of Reynoldsburg, Ohio. The national organization links people who have a heart to minister through dance. CDF has a coordinator in every state. These members come together through conferences, concerts, meetings, fellowships and newsletters. Their focus is the same as the National Liturgical Dance Network.

The International Christian Dance Fellowship (ICDF) is under the direction of several CDF coordinators. The main coordinator is Lucy Andrew—Park Jarasius of Sydney, Australia. This organization links dancers from different cultures, denominations and ministries from all over the world. Twenty—five countries and each continent are represented. When this organization gives a conference or workshop, it is an awesome experience because different cultural dances are taught. Some of these dances are Latin, African, Malaysian, Hawaiian, Japanese, Scottish, Irish, Jewish, Jamaican, Bahamian, etc.

These organizations and many others help get the word and message out about dance ministries and the rightful place that they have in worship services and in God's overall plan. These representatives go all over the world educating pastors and churches about dance ministry protocol and how one should operate. They are most definitely going into all the nations and proclaiming that Jesus is Lord through dance as instructed in Matthew 28. God does not say that it has to be done a certain way; He just wants it done however people can naturally express it. He gives us free will and a variety of gifts. The bottom line is that He wants our praise and worship and as many souls saved before Jesus Christ comes back.

Conclusion

Dance has always been a part of God's original plan when Lucifer was in heaven praising Him with music, instruments and dance. Unfortunately, Lucifer got puffy and wanted all of the glory for himself. God threw him out of heaven and the order of His original plan got radically changed by Lucifer. He started duplicating what was done in heaven, confusing people by making dance appear sensual and evil and taking people's focus off the truth. He made sure that the leaders were not teaching the truth about dance in the church. This is confusion, and God is not the author of confusion.

In the 80's, people's passion to dance began to move slowly into the churches when the knowledge about it from a biblical standpoint was revealed. People began to recognize their call to minister through dance, books began to be published, research was documented and dance teams and ministries were formed. In the latter 90's, mega church ministries began to incorporate dance groups during their TV broadcast. The popular gospel recording artists began to hire dancers to be in their music videos and tour with them during concerts. This got the word out that dancing in the church for Christ was apparently acceptable.

Even though liturgical dance is more visible on TV, in concerts, events, celebrations, worship services, weddings, funerals, birthday parties, etc., some people still do not accept it. When the question was asked at the beginning of this book, "Is Dance Fully Accepted in the Church Today," it was focusing on the word, <u>Church.</u> The word church relates to the Christian faith and beliefs. This was revealed when the liturgical dance surveys were given to church representatives from different denominations. Some of them do not believe in the Christian faith or use the word church for their place of worship. Some use Mosques or Synagogues. Their cultures or doctrines do not allow music or dance to be done during worship. Even the Christian churches did not believe in dance being done at church. Some were honestly not aware of the rapid growth of liturgical dance around the world because some of their denominations are not on TV. They do not go to events that incorporate liturgical dance. They have different books other than the Bible to study. Their books do not mention dance.

The Bible states in Jeremiah 31:13 that the young, old, men and women will be rejoicing in the dance. We are fulfilling that prophecy now with dance ministries, teams and evangelistic groups going all over the world and ministering dance. The word in this passage relates to the church (bride/virgin). It did not say all churches, just the church in general. It did not say all religions that do not believe in Christian doctrines. To answer the question, "Is Dance Fully Accepted in the Church Today?" I would have to say No, not *Fully* accepted. But to the churches that do accept dance: a dance ministry can be an intricate part of their worship service and a major blessing with the right leader and members, protocol, training and biblical knowledge. It will definitely bring the word of God to life, and salvation and deliverance to people through its presentation of movement, music, drama and spoken word with the guidance of the Holy Spirit. I hope that this book was very informative for any ministry or leader released by God to start and maintain a dance ministry. It was truly an honor to share with you my experiences, research, scriptures, words of encouragement and instructions from God. I hope that you will be able to integrate some of the information in your ministry. Be blessed and dance for God with all of your might such as David!

Endnotes

Chapter 1

1. *Holy Bible-King James Version.* (Nashville: Holman Bible Publishers, 1982), Jeremiah 31:13.

2. *The American Heritage Dictionary of the English Language.* Morris, William, Editor. (Boston: Houghton Mifflin Company, 1980), p. 334.

3. Wales, Jimmy, Sanger, Larry. Wikipedia, The Free Encyclopedia (Internet). 2001, p. 2.

4. Dutts, Lorelei. "Celebrate Black History Month-Teach Students about African Contributions to Dance". *Dance Teacher.* Vol. 27, Number 2, (New York: Lifestyle Media, Inc. 2005) pp. 54–55.

5. Butler, Stephanie. *My Body is the Temple-Encounters and Revelations of Sacred Dance and Artistry.* (Fairfax: Xulon Press, 2002), pp. 47–48.

6. *Holy Bible-King James Version.* (Nashville: Holman Bible Publishers, 1982), 1 Chronicles 15:16.

7. Ibid., 2 Chronicles 20:21–22.

8. Ibid., Psalms 150:-1–6.

9. Ibid., Colossians 1:9–12.

10. Rutherford, Pamela. *Make His Praise Glorious.* (Plano), pp. 6–7.

11. *Holy Bible-King James Version.* (Nashville: Holman Bible Publishers, 1982), Lamentations 5:15.

12. Ibid., Isaiah 16:10a.

13. Ibid., Matthew 13:39.

14. Ibid., Revelations 19:7–8.

15. Ibid., Revelations 16:15–16.

16. Ibid., Matthew 28:19–20.

17. Ibid., Psalms 135:2.

18. Ibid., Psalms 95:6

19. Ibid., Isaiah 45:23.

20. Ibid., Psalms 28:2.

21. Ibid., Lamentations 3:30–41.

22. Ibid., Psalms 141:2.

23. Ibid., Psalms 63:4.

24. Ibid., Psalms 44:20.

25. Ibid., Psalms 143:6.

26. Ibid., Exodus 17:11–12.

27. Ibid., Exodus 14:16.

28. Ibid., Psalms 119:48.

29. Ibid., Luke 24:50.

30. Ibid., Daniel 12:7.

31. Ibid., Hebrews 12:12.

32. Ibid., Isaiah 55:12.

33. Ibid., 2 Kings 11:12.

34. Ibid., Psalms 47:1.

35. Ibid., Ezekiel 21:17.

36. Ibid., Job 27:23.

37. Ibid., Ezekiel 6:11.

38. Ibid., Exodus 15:19–21.

39. Ibid., Psalms 149:1–9

40. Kovacs, Aimee Ph.D. *Dancing Into The Anointing.* (Shippensburg: Treasure House, An Imprint of Destiny Image Publishers, Inc., 1996), p. 42.

41. Butler, Stephanie. *My Body is the Temple-Encounters and Revelations of Sacred Dance and Artistry.* (Fairfax: Xulon Press, 2002), p. 169.

42. *Holy Bible-King James Version.* (Nashville: Holman Bible Publishers, 1982), Romans 16:20.

43. Ibid., Isaiah 66:8.

44. Ibid., Psalms 68:24–25.

45. Ibid., Psalms 42:7.

46. Ibid., 1 Corinthians 10:31.

47. Boschman, Lamar. *The Heart of Worship.* (Lake Mary: Charisma House, 1994) p. 122.

48. Strong, James LL.D., S.T.D. *The Strongest Strong's Exhaustive Concordance of the Bible.* 21st Century Edition, (Grand Rapids: Zondervan, 2001).

Chapter 2

1. *Holy Bible-King James Version.* (Nashville: Holman Bible Publishers, 1982), Romans 11:36.

2. Ibid., Colossians 1:16.

3. Ibid., Ezekiel 28:13–15.

4. Ibid., Revelation 4:11.

5. Ibid., Isaiah 61:1–2.

6. Ibid., Jeremiah 31:4.

7.   Ibid., 1 Thessalonians 5:16–18.

8.   Ibid., Psalms 100:4.

9.   Ibid., Psalms 96:8.

10. Ibid., Hebrews 13:15.

11. Ibid., John 4:23–24.

12. *Holy Bible-King James Version.* (Nashville: Holman Bible Publishers, 1982), Genesis 1:1–3.

13. Butler, Stephanie. *My Body is the Temple-Encounters and Revelations of Sacred Dance and Artistry.* (Fairfax: Xulon Press, 2002), p. 49.

14. Garies, Alison. *Warriors of Praise-An Instructional Notebook about Dancing Before the Lord.* (Orange: West Coast Pageantry, 1998) p. 72.

15. Chagrin Valley Web Directory. WebDezign.com. (Chagrin Falls: Moriah Ministries, 2001–2005), p. 2.

16. Rutherford, Pamela. *Make His Praise Glorious.* (Plano), p. 89.

17. *Holy Bible-King James Version.* (Nashville: Holman Bible Publishers, 1982), Job 21:11–12.

18. Ibid., Matthew 11:16–17.

19. Ibid., Judges 11:34.

20. Ibid., Judges 21:20–21.

21. Ibid., 2 Samuel 6:14.

22. Ibid., 2 Chronicles 20:21–22.

23. Ibid., Matthew 14:6–8.

24. Ibid., Isaiah 13:21.

25. Ibid., 1 Chronicles 15:14, 16.

26. Ibid., 1 Corinthians 14:31.

27. Ibid., Psalms 102:18.

28. Ibid., Amos 9:11.

29. Ibid., Acts 3:20–21.

Chapter 3

1.   *Holy Bible-King James Version.* (Nashville: Holman Bible Publishers, 1982), Jeremiah 1:5.

2.   Ibid., 1 Samuel 3:8–10.

3.   Ibid., Ephesians 4:11–13.

Chapter 4

1.   *Holy Bible-King James Version.* (Nashville: Holman Bible Publishers, 1982), Psalms 104:1–2.

2.   Ibid., Isaiah 52:1.

3.   Ibid., Isaiah 61:10.

4.   Butler, Stephanie. *My Body is the Temple-Encounters and Revelations of Sacred Dance and Artistry.* (Fairfax: Xulon Press, 2002), pp. 121–130.

5.   *Holy Bible-King James Version.* (Nashville: Holman Bible Publishers, 1982), Proverbs 18:16.

6.   Ibid., Matthew 28:19–20.

Appendices

1

Facilitator—Dr. Denita Hedgeman

Dance Definition—To move the body rhythmically to music. To leap and skip about or to bob up and down. A series of rhythmical motions and steps, usually to music. (*American Heritage Dictionary*)

Liturgical Dance—Dancing during public worship in the Christian church. *(American Heritage Dictionary)* Where are we to worship/dance God? (Psalms 150) When are we to worship/dance? (Eccl. 3:4) Will of God (I Thess. 5:16–23)

Types—Praise dance/worship dance/sacred dance/dance chorus/dance chorales/Davidic dancers/dance dramatists

Two major functions of liturgical dance: *It tells a story and it gives bodily shape to gratitude or joy.* (page 64) Other functions in the church are:

- **Ministry Unto the Lord**—As worshipers, it is our first priority to use expressive worship/dance as a way to convey our love to the Lord. Romans 12:1–2
- **Ushering in the Presence of the Lord**—The dancers work hand in hand in hand with the singers and musicians. We work corporately to prepare the atmosphere and invite in the Lord's presence. King David used singing, dancing and musical instruments to bring the Ark of the Covenant back to Jerusalem. (II Samuel 6) The dance also prepares the atmosphere for the Holy Spirit to move, especially in the prophetic. Dance/worship sets the atmosphere and once the Holy Spirit comes in, it shifts the atmosphere.
- **To Perform Spiritual Warfare**—The Word connects dance and warfare many times throughout the Bible. Jehoshophat sent out the singers and "those who should praise" the beauty of His holiness into battle first. (II Chron. 20) Our bodies are also weapons according Romans 6:13. It tells us to "present our members (arms/legs) as instruments (weapons) of righteousness to God."
- **To Help Lead the People into His Presence**—Since dancers/singers are worship leaders, they are to help bring people in His Presence. Many times, this is accomplished because of the warfare that they have done. Dancers/worshipers are not there for people to spectate or to entertain, they are there to lead people into participating into worship. Sometimes when people see the worshipers raise their hands, they will do the same. (Psalms 149) (Isaiah 29:13–14)
- **Intercessory Prayer**—Sometimes dance can be used as a prayer of faith, supplication or deliverance. When people are ushered into the presence of God, they are no longer spectating, usually worship, repentance, forgiveness and

change come as the dancers pray to God through their dance. (Col. 1:9–16)

- **Special Presentations**—There are times when the Lord gives us a special song/dance to prepare for presentation to the congregation or special meetings. These may be group or solo dances. These are usually prophetic dances, in the sense of their timing. He has us do certain dances at certain times for specific reasons. A dance presentation should have the same effect as a preacher's sermon—to encourage the saints, as well as, the sinners to love God enough to desire to please Him. (I Cor. 10:31) Dances can be spontaneous or choreographed.

Worship with movement is an attitude of love expressed actively. Expressive movement is an act of our wills in worship to the Lord. Movements are invested with meaning because human beings have bodies and spirits. (page 63)

What are some natural expressions of movements that we do naturally? In the congregation?

Forms of Dance—Secular

Ballet	Jazz	Tap
Hip—Hop	Aerobics	Modern Cultural
Line Dancing	Party	Pilates

Types of Liturgical Dance

Celebration	Praise	Warfare
Processional	Interpretative	Prophetic
Spontaneous	Travail	Worship
Flags	Banners	Tambourines
Mime	Drama	Festivals
Jewish (Circles)	Restoration	

Hebrew Praises

Yadah—Worship with an extended hand. (2 Chron. 20:19–21; Psalms 63:4, 134:2, 141:2; 1 Tim. 2:8)

Towdah— An extension of the hand in adoration, sacrifice or adoration. (2 Chron. 29:31; Jer. 30:19; Ps. 26:7 & 50:14)

Halah— Root word from hallelujah meaning to boast, brag, shine, celebrate. (Ps. 104, 105, 106)

Shabach— To address in a loud tone, to command, triumph, glory, or shout. (Ps. 63:1, 3, 4; 117:1, 47:1, 35:27; 106:47)

Barak— To kneel or bow down. (Ps. 95:6; 1 Chron. 29:20 and Neh. 9:5)

Zamar—Praise God with music and instruments. Psalm 150, 21:3, 66:2, 4; Is. 12:5)

Tehillah— To sing or laud. (Ps. 22:3; I Chron. 16:35; Is. 42:10, 12; II Chron. 20:22)

Old Testament Dances
Worship   Celebrations   Warfare   Festivals   Restoration

New Testament Dances
Celebrations   Evil (seductive)   Healing   Faith

People Who Danced in the Bible Children (Mat. 11:16–17)
Women (Judges 11:34, 21:20–21; Ex. 15:20–1st mention of dance in the Bible)

David (II Sam. 6:12–23; I Sam. 29:5; I Chron. 15:25–29; I Sam. 18:6)

Worshipers (Psalms 149:3)

Joyful Dance (Ps. 30:11)

Evil Dance Ex. 32:19; Mark 6:22–23; Mat. 14:6

Dance to Greet a Son's Returning (Luke 15:21–25)

Healing of Lame Man (Acts 3:1–10)

Dance of Restoration (Jer. 31:4, 13)

The original purpose of dance was to dance and praise God in the sanctuary until satan took it and replicated to the world and made it lustful. (Restoring the Dance by Ann Stevenson chapter 3/p. 16; Ez. 28:13–19; Is. 14:12; Rom. 11:36

Restoration of all things—Acts 3:20–21

2

PRAISE DANCE PREPARATORY WORKSHOP

FACILATATOR—DR. DENITA HEDGEMAN, MINISTER OF DANCE

PRAY THE WORD! DANCE THE WORD! LIVE THE WORD!

Introduction of Facilitator
Introduction of Attendees/Prayer Requests
Prayer
Format—Bible Study/Warm – ups/Dance Routines

Discussion: Do You Have A Passion To Serve The Lord Through Dance?

Are You Truly Called To *Minister* Through Dance?

Will of God—I Thess. 5:16–23; Psalms 149; Psalms 150—handout

Praise expresses admiration, appreciation and thanksgiving!

A dance presentation should have the same effect as a preacher's sermon—to encourage the saints, as well as, the sinners to love God enough to desire to please Him. I Cor. 10:31; Col. 1:9–14

Jesus' Mission Statement to Ministry—A Dancer's/Minister's Mission Statement—Isaiah 61

Dance is to move the body and feet in rhythm to music. It expresses joy, freedom, victory, pleasure and a time of celebration.—Handout

Original purpose of dance was to dance and praise God in the Sanctuary until Satan took it and replicated to the world and made it lustful. Ezek. 28:13–19; Isa. 14:12; Rom. 11:36

Types of Dances

Celebration	Prophetic	Choreodrama	Praise
Travail	Offering	Warfare	Worship
Sermonic	Processional	Flags/Streamers	
Communion			
Interpretative	Tambourines	Pantomime	Banners
Sign Language	Spoken Word		

Hebrew Praises

Towdah—Sacrifice/Adoration   Yadah—Lift hands
Shabach—Shout   Zamar—Play instruments
Barouch—Bow   Hallel—Boast or brag
Tehillah—Sing/Laud

People Who Danced in The Bible

Children (Mat. 11:16–17)

Women (Judges 11:34, 21:20–21 & Exodus 15:20)

David (II Sam. 6:12–23; I Sam. 29:5; I Chron. 15:25–29; & I Sam. 18:6)

Worshippers (149:3)

Joyful Dance (Psalms 30:11)

Evil Dance (Exodus 32:19; Mark 6:22–23 & Mat. 14:6)

Dance to Express Joy in Victory (I Sam. 18:6–7)

Dance to Greet a Son's Returning (Luke 15:21–25)

Dance of Rejoicing in the Lord (II Sam. 6:14, 16)

Dance in the Last Days (Jeremiah 31:13)

Dance of Restoration and Healing (Jeremiah 31:4, 13 & Acts 3:1–16)

Getting Fit For Praise Dancing

I.   *Scriptural Reference*
       Eccl. 3:4

II.   *Instructional Learning*
      A.   *Taking Care Of Physical Body*—Eating right, rest, technique classes, etc. (Gen. 1:29, I Tim. 4:4)

           Technique—(II Tim. 2:15) Do your best to win God's approval as a worker who does not need to be ashamed and who only teaches the true message.

           Dance is a visual art form that does require a certain amount of technique. Technique (as defined by The Merriam Webster dictionary) is the manner in which technical details are treated or basic physical movements are used.

           Improving your technique will allow you to deliver God's messages of love, deliverance, salvation, and forgiveness more effectively. It will also free you from becoming a stumbling block to someone else. Never allow yourself to become an excuse for someone else. Always be willing to improve so that others around you will rise and improve also.

           Keep in mind, even though technique is important, it is not the most important aspect in dance ministry. The *Anointing* is the most important aspect of dance ministry.

B. *Taking Care of Your Spiritual Body*—Mind and Spirit (Psalms 51:10, Rom. 12:1–2 & I Cor. 6:19–20 & II Cor. 7:1)

III. C. *Presentation*

D. *Demonstrating Charisma, Pose and Confidence* (II Tim. 2:21, Psalms 45:3, Esther 8:15, & Luke 16:19)

Pray The Word!
Jeremiah 29:11–14/Matthew 7:7–8

Dance The Word!
Psalms 23/Psalms 91

Live The Word!
James 1:22–23

Management/participation of an Effective Dance Ministry

- You are responsible and held accountable for what your ministry does.
- Pray, meditate and ask God to show you what message He wants to convey to His people, what music to use, how to do it and what should the dancers wear.
- Once He tells you, don't waver! (James 1:5–8)
- Pray for wisdom not to offend anyone with your presentation (Rom. 14)
- Educate your congregation, especially if you come from a traditional church (Have a narration or scripture reading before the dance, have the words printed in the bulletin or invite another ministry to perform.
- Conduct auditions, admittance requirements or standard rules.

- Have dancers prepare spiritually before the dance. (Bible study, prayer, meditation, fasting, & anointing with oil)
- Know what your true purpose is, strengths and how you are going to enhance the ministry.
- Be flexible! You might have to do something different at the last minute or the Holy Spirit could lead you into prophetic dancing.
- Be focused before ministering by going to a quiet place alone to meditate, warm—up and rehearse.
- Go the extra mile by studying parallel scriptures; working out in other sports; taking acting and dance classes; attending workshops; participating in other productions; renting movies or going to plays that are related to your character; playing the music without dancing so you will know every part of the dance in your mind, etc.

3

Processionals

What truth are we declaring as we process?

Processionals do not exalt a man; They exalt God.

What props will you use (Banners, Flags, Streamers, Tambourines, etc.)?

Psalms 24:7; 68:24; II Cor. 2:14

Flags/banners In The Bible

Flags wave God's blessings unto the congregation.

Billow Banners—Covering of the Lord. When you sit, pray or dance under it, you are in presence of the Lord (Holy of Holies) Psalms 42:7

Streamers wave and sweep God's blessings over the congregation. Psalms 42:7

Tribal and Family Banners: Numbers 2:2; 10:10–14

Warfare: Psalms 20:5; 74:4; Isaiah 31:9; Song of Solomon 6:4

A Rallying Point: Isaiah 5:26; 11:10

As Proclamation: Jeremiah 4:6; 51:12; Isaiah 62:10; Psalms 60:4

Tambourines

The tambourine was used in warfare and to celebrate victory: Exodus 15:20; I Sam. 18:6; Judges 11:34

The tambourine was used in Praise and Worship: 1 Sam. 10:5; 2 Sam. 6:5; I Chron. 13:8; Psalms 68:25; 81:2; 149:3; 150:4; Jer. 31:4

Praise Garments/garments Of Praise—Psalms 104:2

Each small part of the High Priest's garment represents some facet of truth or identification. The garments were given by God to communicate glory and beauty. Isaiah 52:1

Ephod—The most important item of the priestly clothing. A kind of apron made of materials woven out of gold and linen thread and variously colored yarns. It covered the back and chest, reaching nearly to the knees. It fastened to the body by two straps and a belt with which it was lined. (Linen, gold, blue, purple & scarlet)
The tunic was worn under the outer garment. Ex. 28:39

The materials were to be made from materials received in offerings from the people. Ex. 25:2–7

Instructions for the garments—Ex. 28 & 29

Preparation of the garments—Ex. 39:1–31

4

Denomination: **Church:**

Pastor: **Survey Participant:**

1. What is Liturgical Dance?

2. Is liturgical dance a part of your church or denomination? If so, what type of dance or groups do you have?

3. What do you think is God's view on liturgical dance in the church?

4. What do you think is the universal church's view on liturgical dance?

5. Despite your personal belief's, why do you think liturgical dance is growing rapidly around the world?

6. Who was the first person that danced in the Bible?

7. What is the sole purpose of a dance ministry?

8. Do you see it as entertainment or ministry?

9. Can souls get saved through liturgical dance?

10. Is liturgical dance fully accepted in the church?

5

MBCC MISSION STATEMENT (UNTIL 2004)

By faith, we seek to be a spirit—led urban church developing fully mature followers of Christ, touching and transforming the world through the presence of God.

The Call To Praise Dance—Walk Worthy of your Vocation (Ephesians 4)

1.   Ability—1 Peter 4:10–11
    a.   Gifted or Developed Talent
    b.   Inward Desire, Will, Passion to Dance

2.   Consistency is a key word in the life of a Praise Dancer. It brings results every time.
    a.   Prayer, Praise and Practice—Establish set times for these and stick to them.
    b.   Daniel prayed three times a day, was not distracted, was delivered and God received the glory. (Daniel 6)

3.   Dedication and Commitment to God is top priority. You must not let anything, anyone or any activity hinder you from the commitment you have made to God to complete the work that he has begun in you. *This is Your Ministry!*

a. Noah—120 years to build the ark.

4. Confidence is God's Plan and Purpose for your life. Self—confidence is ineffective. Our confidence must lie in the hands and direction of God.
   a. We can do nothing without God—John 15:5
   b. We must depend on God to lead and guide us—Acts 17:28

5. Humility is a must! The goal is to draw men unto God.
   a. Confidence in God elevates humility.
   b. We now recognize that our abilities and gifts come from God and are in His hands.
   c. Submit to His will.

6. Complete Sacrifice requires total self—denial. The total man must be surrendered to God, body mind and spirit, so that he can flow through you and bring forth awesome praise.
   a. Don't settle for mediocre
   b. Living sacrifice—Romans 12:1–2

7. Focus on the goal. Remember the goal is to allow God to fulfill this ministry in you.
   a. Keep your eye on the goal no matter what.
   b. Paul never lost his focus on God from the time he was called on the road to Damascus—He went through every type of situation.
   c. 2 Timothy 4:6, 7 & 8

6

The Dance Ministry will hold open enrollment and auditions during the month of October. If you are between the ages of 8 years old and adult, a member of our church and have a zeal to dance for the Lord, this might be the ministry for you. You must have the following prepared for the audition: a 32 count dance routine, a two paragraph statement on your relationship with God and how you will incorporate it into the ministry, and the ability to learn a dance combination. You may sign—up at the registration table outside the bookstore after worship service on Sunday, September 26, 2004.

7

DANCE MINISTRY

SIGN—UP

8

DANCE MINISTRY REQUIREMENTS

- Baptized believer and member of MBCC Church!
- Active in a Bible study and pursuing a worship relationship with god!
- Experience in dance/acting/signing/tumbling!
- Experience in ministering/performing with personality in front of an audience!
- 8 Years old to adult! (Please boys & men are welcome)
- Prepare a 32 count dance routine!
- Two paragragh essay on your relationship with god and how you are going to incorporate it in the ministry!
- Be required to attend a series of preparatory workshops before released to minister!

Also needed:
- Seamtresses/costume designers
- Stage/prop/worship production assistants
- Artists/sign designers
- Narrators
- Computer/administrative assistants
- Prayer warriors/devotion leaders
- Sponsors/fundraisers

9

MISSISSIPPI BOULEVARD CHRISTIAN CHURCH

DANCE MINISTRY SIGN—UP

NAME/ ADDRESS/ZIP	PARENT'S NAME	TELEPHONE/ E-MAIL	YOUTH AGE/ ADULT	YEARS OF TRAINING/ WHAT AREA

10

MBCC DANCE MINISTRY REGISTRATION FORM

First Name	Last Name	M.I.

Parent's First Name	Last Name	M.I.

Address

City	State	Zip Code

( )	( )	( )
Home Phone #	Work Phone #	Cellular Phone #

E-Mail Address	Age (Optional for Adults)	Grade

[ ] Girl   [ ] Boy   [ ] Female   [ ]   Male

How many years of dance experience do you have?
[ ]   0-2 years   [ ]   3-5 years   [ ]   5 & up

Please list other performing arts experience _____

Why do you want to be a part of the dance ministry? _____

How would the dance ministry benefit from you being a part? _____

How would you benefit from being a part of the ministry? _____

Are you an active member of a bible study? Is so, list the name of the class _____

List any illnesses, allergies or medicines

For traveling or outside ministry opportunities, please name insurance carrier, ID# & physician information

Emergency Contact Information

Name	Phone #	Relationship

Audition Requirements
[ ] Registration Form   [ ] Two Paragraph Essay   [ ] 32 Count Routine

1 1

October 2, 2004
        Auditions   4th Floor   1:00 p.m.—3:00 p.m.

October 9, 2004
        Workshop I   4th Floor   1:00 p.m.—3:00 p.m.

October 16, 2004
        Workshop II   4th Floor   1:00 p.m.—3:00 p.m.

If you have completed both workshops, you may start coming to regular rehearsals with the returning dance ministry members. You must start reading "Dancing Into The Anointing", take exam, and purchase new praise garments before you can minister.

This orientation period may take up to a month and half to complete. Most dance ministries have a 3 month to 6 month probation period.

12

DANCE MINISTRY AUDITIONS

SATURDAY, OCTOBER 2, 2004

TIME	NAME	TECHNIQUE/ PERSONALITY	MATERIAL	RATING 1-5
1:00 P.M.				
1:10 P.M.				
1:20 P.M.				
1:30 P.M.				
1:40 P.M.				
1:50 P.M.				
2:00 P.M.				
2:10 P.M.				
2:20 P.M.				
2:20 P.M.				
2:30 P.M.				
2:40 P.M.				
2:50 P.M.				
3:00 P.M.				

13

Dance Ministry Church Extension— (901) 729–6222 #415–
(Information changed weekly)

Rehearsals   Saturday—11:00 a.m. until 2:00 p.m.
                              Extra rehearsals may be expected during the week
                              of a scheduled ministry performance.

Operational Months of Ministry—September until June of follow-ing year—Break in summer—A dancer cannot be pulled in and out of the ministry during the year unless it is an emergency and the Minister of Dance/Director fully knows the circumstances.—No surprises!

- Dance Ministry usually performs once a month or when requested by church leaders, the worship committee or other ministries.

- Dance Ministry occasionally accepts outside engagements such as weddings, community worship services, retirement celebra-tions, family reunions, etc. We will start ministering at the nursing homes, orphanages, hospitals, charities, etc.

Praise Garments (Costumes)

Females—

> White long sleeve unitard, white long skirt and black ballet shoes.
>
> Purchased at Barbara's Dancewear, 1499 S. Perkins, 38117–682–6898 (Ask her for the MBCC discount)
>
> Mid—South Dancewear, Inc., 7014 E. Shelby Drive, 38125–751–6737
>
> You need to order costumes *ASAP* because it takes a couple weeks for them to come.
>
> Rainbow *colored dress of your choice*
>
> *Purple top and palazzo pants*
>
> Purchased through Lady Di in Dallas, TX—Costume Committee with handle orders/measurements.

Males —

> White short sleeve t—shirt, Black short sleeve t—shirt, white pants, black pants and black jazz capezio shoes.
>
> *Purple long sleeved tunics and colorful long sleeve shirts of your choice*—See Costume Committee.

(Occasionally, we will wear ephods like David wore and other biblical garments to accessorize our basic praise garments. Also, prayer shawls, scarves, flags, banners, billow banners, etc.)

Class Format

Prayer Requests/Praise Reports—*Please bring Bible, assigned book, a pen, writing paper & folder—Mandatory*

Prayer

Bible Study

Ballet Warm—up

Locomotive Movements

Routine

Prayer

Assigned Books for 2004–2005

Dancing Into The Anointing by Aimee Kovacs, Ph.D.

Restoring The Dance by Ann Stevenson

My Body Is A Temple by Rev. Stephanie Butler

Expectations

- Each dancer is expected to be on time for rehearsals so everyone can leave on time.

- A dancer is excused for only two missed **consecutive** rehearsals if he or she calls the ministry leader. A dancer cannot participate in an upcoming performance if he or she does not call and misses two consecutive rehearsals. A dancer cannot miss the week of and the rehearsal before a performance unless it is an emergency and is brought to the ministry leader's attention. *Always communicate with the ministry leader in advance and you will probably be excused.*

- No gum chewing

- Each female dancer is expected to wear her hair pulled back in a bun for a liturgical performance unless otherwise instructed.

- Each dancer should come to class properly dressed and stretched out individually while waiting on the class to begin.

- Each dancer should have their dance shoes for class. *Do not wear tennis shoes in class.*

Officers

We will have a small pool of officers to assist with some decisions and the overall flow of the ministry—especially when the Minister of Dance/Director is absent due to sickness, class, out of town or other ministry engagements. The officers will be:

Assistant Director

Secretary/Treasurer

Praise Garment Committee Representative

Parent Representative

Child Dance Captain

Youth Dance Captain

Adult Dance Captain

During the first year, the Minister of Dance/Director will choose the officers based on God's leading, commitment, talent, skill level and walk with God. The officers will be voted on and chosen by the Dance Ministry Team after the first year.

Demerit System
There will be a demerit system this year. Since the number five represents grace in the Bible, you have up to five demerits before you will be asked to sit down from the ministry for a restoration period until further decided by the Minister of Dance and Officers. A demerit will be given due to discipline problems, excessive talking/lateness, unexcused missed rehearsals, talking while in hall of the sanctuary before ministering, rudeness to fellow dance member, not bringing Bible, book, paper, pen and folder, etc. When you are allowed to come back to the ministry, you have to attend three consecutive rehearsals before you can minister again with the group.

Progress Reports (Verbal or Written)
From time to time, the Minister of Dance/Director will either call parents or adult dancers with a progress report so that everyone is aware of how well they are doing in the ministry or what areas they need to work on. The Minister of Dance/Director is looking at class participation, attitude, personality, if the student has been practicing at home, technique and spiritual growth.

Attendance

Please don't wait until the morning of rehearsal to call the Minister of Dance/Director to tell her that you will not be there or if you are running late. Call her during the week or the night before so she can plan accordingly. Also, make sure you sign the roll when you first come to class. *You are allowed to miss two consecutive unexcused rehearsals. Call the Minister of Dance/Director if you are going to be absent so you will be excused.*

Class Time

It is preferred that parents drop off their child before class and come back to pick them up. No parents should be sitting in class unless they are working on a parent committee and are meeting during that time. Thank you for your cooperation.

Hours

Rehearsals are on Saturdays from 11:00 a.m. until 2:00 p.m. on the 4th floor of the Nursery Building. Sometimes you might be asked to come on Monday nights from 5:30 p.m. until 7:30 p.m. if we are preparing intensely for a ministering engagement or worship service. Usually students' prayer requests and praise reports last more than 10 minutes, so rehearsals might not end exactly at the designated time. We do not want to hinder the spirit, so we will sometimes use a grace period from 10–20 minutes to reflect, pray and make announcements. Occasionally, the Minister of Dance/Director will have parent meetings during that grace time.

Orientation Workshops/Auditions

There will be a formal audition in order to be a part of this performing ministry. Don't audition for a musical dance group without music unless it is a spoken word piece. The two go together. Everyone is graded and rated on all three sections—32 count routine, routine demonstrated by the Minister of Dance/Director and an essay on the dancer's relationship with God and how they are going to incorporate their gifts and calling into the ministry. It is mandatory for new members to attend scheduled orientation workshops. If the student is a child or teenager, their parents have to attend with them to get a better understanding of the ministry and requirements. New members have to wait before they can officially participate with the ministry for two months. This will give you time to get acclimated to everything, Bible study, order and get praise garments made, come to class and build technique and know if this ministry really fits your calling.

Conferences/Retreat/Concert
Once a year, there will be a Dance Ministry concert in June. Each year the ministry will attend a mandatory conference in or out of the city or a year—end retreat decided by the Minister of Dance/Director.

Praise Garment/Prop Fee
There is $20.00 praise garment fee required per semester for the buying, renting and usage of new/old props and praise garment accessories. (Required on the first class of the new season in September and on the first class in January) $30.00 for two people per family and extra $10.00 for each additional family member

Fundraising
If the church approves, we will sometimes have fundraising activities decided by Minister of Dance/Director and Officers.

Fasting
The night before each performance, the dance ministry is asked to fast and pray for unity, clarity, the anointing and the receptiveness of the congregation so that the message of the dance is well received. We will fast from 6:00 p.m. until 6:00 a.m. the next morning. During your fast you should pray, study the provided scriptures, not attend slumber parties, movies, talk on the telephone, plan secular events, etc. If you feel led to look at TV or talk on the telephone, look at something spiritual or talk to a prayer partner concerning the ministry. Sometimes it is good just to be quiet and meditate so

you can hear the small still voice of God. God might decide to do something totally different the next day and the ministry needs to be on one accord.

Day of Worship Service or Event

Members of the Dance Ministry should be in the sanctuary at 7:00 a.m. to pray and go over last minute spacing and choreography. It is important that you are on time, because by 7:20 a.m. other people involved in the worship service start to come in the sanctuary to prepare for their part as well. We need to be downstairs in the dressing rooms changing no later than 7:30 a.m. Our usual dressing rooms are the groomsman's room in the Fellowship Hall and the bridal room across from the chapel. Since we have more dancers that the dressing rooms can hold, sometimes there will be additional assigned rooms for you. Please remain quiet in the Fellowship Hall because there are Sunday School classes in session and the people and ushers can hear us. Let's be mindful and prayerful. After first, service, the ministry will to into the balcony and participate in the worship service as a group. Please change quickly after you minister, so you won't miss the sermon. Immediately following service, the ministry will come back to the dressing rooms to eat our snacks, then proceed to Sunday School. *Parents and children please don't take food out of the designated areas. Ushers have reported dancers eating upstairs and disturbing communion after they have ministered. After 2nd service, either leave or find parents quietly.* Please be back in the room at 10:30 a.m. to prepare and change for the next service to minister. *Do not leave services unless there is an emergency. We don't want anything to happen to you and you can't get back in time to participate for the next service.* If the church moves to one service, we will still arrive an hour before to pray, prepare and change clothes. Make sure that you already have on your unitard and t—shirts under your street clothes so people won't see your praise garment and that is will be easy to slip on your skirt/pants before you minister. Please put on makeup on and have your hair already in a bun before you come so that won't take up your preparation time and meditation before service. Males should already have on their black/white pants, but later slip their shirts on before they minister. Make sure that you have a t—shirt on under your shirt. Ladies, please put band—aids on your chest under your underwear so the congregation won't see the imprint of your chest in the light. Everyone should wear black underwear. Please don't wear flowered underwear or white under white. If you are full figured, please wear a sleeveless black leotard to go under your white. Also, wear a supportive bra under your outfit. We will still wear the white unitard under the rainbow dresses and purple outfits. Each participant is asked to bring healthy light snacks between services. There will be a sign—up sheet the rehearsal before we minister so you can designate what you are going to bring. Remember, we have about 50 people involved. Sometimes you will be responsible for bring a snack for yourself and not the ministry. Please remember to clean up your dressing room after the performance.

Please don't forget to take your items home and put your name on your shoes, tags, books, Bibles, belongings, etc.

I, _____,
comply with the rules and guidelines of the Mississippi Boulevard
Christian Church Dance Ministry. I am obligated to participate
with the ministry for at least a year. (Not breaking up the year
without telling the Minister of Dance/Director due to grades or
other activities) I know that this is God's ministry and I want to
give Him my all and seriousness like I do for other outside secu-
lar/school activities. I promise to communicate with the Minister
of Dance/Director if my schedule changes in plenty of enough
time. I will bring positiveness, cooperation, encouragement,
skill, prayer, gifts and anointing to this ministry.

_____   _____
Signature   **Date**

_____   _____
Parent's Signature   **Date**

14

DANCE MINISTRY ROLL

LAST	FIRST	4/20/04	4/27/04	5/8/04	5/15/04	5/22/04	5/29/04	6/5/04	6/8/04

15

MISSISSIPPI BOULEVARD CHRISTIAN CHURCH TELEPHONE LIST

NAME	PARENT'S NAME	ADDRESS/ZIP/E-MAIL	TELEPHONE

16

DANCE MINISTRY DEMERIT SYSTEM

LAST	FIRST	#1 REASON	#2 REASON	#3 REASON	#4 REASON	#5 REASON	RESULTS

A. Lateness

B. Unexcused Absences

C. Gum Chewing

D. Excessive Talking During Class

E. Attitude

F. Excessive Talking Before/During Service

G. Disrespect Against Assigned Leader

H. Does Not Know Dance After Weeks of Practice

I. Not Turning Forms/Money on Time

J. No Ballet Shoes/Hair Not in Bun/Wearing Earrings

K. Does Not Have Bible/Book/Paper/Pen

17

MBCC DANCE MINISTRY

Progress Report

Name: _____

Attendance: _____
_____
_____

Attitude: _____
_____
_____

Ability to Learn Dances/Assignments: _____
_____
_____

Participation in Bible Study: _____
_____
_____

Ministry Growth: _____

_____

_____

Technique Growth: _____

_____

_____

Focus: _____

_____

_____

Cooperation: _____

_____

_____

Does Everything Assigned in a Timely Manner: _____

_____

_____

_____

Participation in Outside Events (Conferences/Retreats, etc.:)

_____

_____

_____

18

MBCC DANCE MINISTRY

Prayer Request

Name _____

_____

_____

_____

_____

_____

_____

Praise Report

Name _____

_____

_____

_____

_____

_____

_____

19

BIBLE STUDY NOTE SUMMARY
DANCE MINISTRY

Date:
Book/Chapter:
Scripture:

Main Points

1.

2.

3.

4.

5.

6.

7.

8.

9.

10.

Main Idea

20

January 17, 2004
Isaiah 61:1–3
Jesus' and your mission statement as a ministry!

Read verses 1–3

- In order for God to pour out His spirit or for anything to happen, there should be a belief in Christ and His death, burial, and resurrection on your behalf must take place.

- Next, there should be a baptism of water (salvation)—Exception of the order is in Acts 10.

- For those who are willing to receive, there come the promises and actions of Isaiah 61.

    1. The spirit of the Lord is upon you! What does *upon you* mean?

    2. What does *anointed* mean?

When God _____ and they receive their _____ _____ the Lord will _____ that person for the particular reason that they have been _____.

Name eight things that God expects us to do after he anoints us.

1.

2.

3.

4.

5.

6.

7.

8.

What dances or activities has Dance Ministry demonstrated these actions and appointments of God?

21

DANCING INTO THE ANOINTING

Introduction

- Look in the front of the book and read the beginning scriptures.

- Read Jeremiah 31 (emphasize v. 12–13)

- Read the purpose section (read different versions of Ephesians 4:13)

- Go over the Introduction section.

    I.   What are the six types of dance and what do they mean?
        a.
        b.
        c.
        d.
        e.
        f.

2.   What occasions are popular for sacred dance?

3.   Where do we dance for the Lord?

During your personal study time, here are some more dance scriptures:

Psalms 68:25 (tambourine dancing)
Psalms 149:3 (Praise Him with the dance)
Psalms 150:4 (Praise Him with the dance/sanctuary)
Ecclesiastes 3:4 (Time to dance)
Psalms 30:11 (mourning into dancing)
Luke 15 (Prodigal Son)
I Samuel 18:6–7 (David)
II Samuel 6:12–23 (Ark of the Covenant)
I Chronicles 15:25–29 (David)
Exodus 15:20 (Celebration of crossing the Red Sea)
Matthew 14:1–12 (Provocative)
I Samuel 29:5 (David)
Jeremiah 31:4 (Dance of restoration)
Jeremiah 31:13 (Dance in the last days)

22

1. What are the six types of dance and what do they mean?
   - a.
   - b.
   - c.
   - d.
   - e.
   - f.

2. What occasions are popular for sacred dance?

3. What does the title "Dancing Into the Anointing" mean?

4. How do you know when you are called?
   - a.
   - b.
   - c.
   - d.

5. What is the Ark of the Covenant?

6. What were the six parts of the David's worship service back then?
   - a.
   - b.
   - c.
   - d.
   - e.
   - f.

7. Name and define the seven Hebrew words for praise.

    a.   e.

    b.   f.

    c.   g.

8. What are the characteristics of a good teacher/leader?

    a.   h.

    b.   i.

    c.   j.

    d.   k.

    f.   l.

    g.

9. What are requirements of a dancer on the team?

    a.   e.

    b.   f.

    c.   g.

    d.   h.

10. What is the correct order or circle of a praise service?

11. What is the reason why the church doesn't see a lot of salvations, healings deliverances and other divine manifestations?

23

PROPOSED DANCE MINISTRY CONCERT COSTS

JUNE 13, 2004

Print Production of Programs	$ 600.00 (for 1000)
Photographer	$ 200.00
Radio Advertisements	$ 40.00 per spot (Natalie is researching quotes)
TVAdvertisements is researching quotes/PSA's)	$ 750.00 & up (Natalie
Radio/TV Emcee Personality	$ 200.00–$300.00 (Natalie is researching quotes)
Postage for Invitations	$ 15.00
Staging from Grand Rental	$ 180.00
Backdrop	$ 600.00
Printing of Flyer Cards	$ 100.00 (Paid in full)
Music Production	$ 75.00
Props/Material to Make Items	$ 300.00
Gifts for Participants	$ 250.00
Choreographer's Honorarium	$ 500.00

Costumes—Children	$ 115.00 @ 33
Costumes—Adults	$ 125.00 @ 10
Total	$3910.00
	(Without number of radio spots and costumes per student added)

*Usually choreographer pays for everything except the printing of programs/photographer and media spots. The church had paid for those.

If we had done the glamour fundraiser, the ministry would have received $2,000 up front with no waiting periods on getting the money to out of town vendors that take weeks to make and ship.

Thank you for you consideration on assisting the Dance Ministry with the concert.

Dr. Denita Hedgeman
Minister of Dance/Choreographer

24

Please start announcing in bulletin and on screens May 9th for volunteers!

Now is the time to exercise your privilege of participation. The Dance Ministry will have a concert on June 13, 2004 at MBCC at 4:00 p.m. in the sanctuary. Volunteers are needed in the following areas:

> Costume Seamstresses
> Stage/Prop Hands
> Artists for Sets & Signs
> Supplies Management
> Security
> Narrators
> Extras
> Male Dancers
> Four Small Dancers Between the Ages of 5–6

If you feel led to assist, call the church at 729–6222 #415 and leave a message.

Please start announcing in bulletin, pulpit and on screens May 23 and 30, June 6 and 13.

Come out and enjoy the Dance Ministry in concert in "Dances of Praise III" on June 13, 2004 at MBCC at 4:00 p.m. in the sanctuary. They will minister ballet, jazz, tap, African jazz, Messianic Jewish, Latin, hip—hop, prophetic, congregational, testimonies, praise and worship, pantomime and drama. Also, other dance ministries and groups will minister such as St. Andrew AME Church, Abundant Grace, Nubian Dance Theater and more! Don't miss this wonderful opportunity to participate and witness the dancers as they dance into the anointing and higher praise!

25

"DANCES OF PRAISE III" CONCERT MEETING

Involved:

MBCC Dance Ministry/Guest Dancers/Two Other Dance Ministries

Facility Req.:

*Sanctuary from 2:00 p.m. until 7:00 p.m.—Set—up/rehearsal/concert/set— down

*Bridal/Groom's Dressing Rooms

*Fellowship Hall and some Classrooms—Holding space & Dressing Rooms for Guest Dancers and Visiting Dance Ministries

*Women's Bathroom outside of sanctuary on the Organ side

*Hallway surrounding Sanctuary on the backside by Pastor's office—Quick Dressing spaces— Curtain off by rented curtains

*Open space outside the hallway on the organ side through the doors by the stairwell

*Open hallway between the Sanctuary and Nursery

*Removal of Pulpit Furniture and Chairs in the Choir Stand

*Table for Glamour You Fundraiser One Sunday After Both Services

*Room for Glamour You Pictures to be Taken/Viewed

**These are the same requests that we had from last year. Nothing has changed.

Church Responsibility Requests:

Printing of Programs—Approximately $600.00–$800.00 (500–1000 #)

Media/Press Releases, PSA's, Paid Advertisements

Assisting with Flyer Duplications and Distributions

Assisting with the Mail—Out of Invitations

Bulletin and Pulpit Announcements of Event

Media/Sound/Video Staff to Assist with Concert/Screen Advertisements MBCC News)

Possible Security of Dancers Valuables in Dressing Rooms—especially Guests

Dance Ministries in Fellowship Hall

Dance Ministry Responsibilities:

Find Out How Much Is in The Dance Ministry Budget

Sponsor a Carwash and Glamour You Fundraisers

Pay for Rental of Staging and Gifts for Participants

Rehearsals:

Every Saturday in April and May from 11:00 a.m. until 2:00 p.m. on the 4th Floor (Same schedule)

Tuesday, April 27, 2004–4th Floor—5:30 p.m. until 7:30 p.m.

Saturday, June 5, 2004–Sanctuary—11:00 a.m. until 2:00 p.m.

*Tuesday, June 8, 2004–Sanctuary—5:30 p.m. until 8:00 p.m.

*Thursday, June 10, 2004–Sanctuary—5:30 p.m. until 7:30 p.m.

Sunday, June 13, 2004–2:00 p.m. until 3:30 p.m.

*Media/Sound/Video Staff needed for rehearsals!

26

The Dance Ministry
of
Mississippi Boulevard Christian Church
Cordially invites you to their
Dance Concert
"Dances Of Praise III"

On
Sunday, June 13, 2004 at 4:00 p.m. in the sanctuary
Admission: Free

Ballet, Jazz, Tap, Interpretive, Latin, Spoken Word, Prophetic,
Congregational, Praise & Worship, Drama, Pantomime, Etc.

Dr. Denita Hedgeman
Director/Principal Choreographer
70 N. Bellevue
Memphis, TN 38104
729–6222 #415

27

May 2, 2004

Erica Anderson
Dance Ministry
Abundant Grace Church
843 W. Raines Road
Memphis, TN 38109

Dear Ms. Anderson:

Your dance ministry is cordially invited to be a featured guest dance ministry in our annual dance ministry concert "Dances of Praise III" June 13, 2004 at 4:00 p.m. at Mississippi Blvd. Christian Church. Our address is 70 N. Bellevue.

We are expecting three other dance ministries to participate during the finale. Each ministry leader is asked to choreograph a section and a half of the dance and learn a combined choreographed section by the MBCC ministry leader, Denita Hedgeman.

I am asking that your group attend the rehearsals on Tuesday, June 8, 2004 from 5:30 p.m. until 8:00 p.m. and Thursday, June 10, 2004 from 5:30 p.m. until 8:00 p.m. in our sanctuary. These rehearsals will include the sound, video, narrators, actors and all dancers. If you can, I would like for you to attend the rehearsal on Saturday, June 5, 2004 from 1:00 p.m.—2:00 p.m. to learn the curtain call.

I am so excited about what God is doing in this collaborated effort. If you have any questions or concerns, please feel free to contact me at the church, (901) 729–6222.

Thank you for your consideration and God bless you and your ministry!

Sincerely,

Denita Hedgeman

Denita Hedgeman
Minister of Dance/Choreographer
Mississippi Blvd. Christian Church Dance Ministry

28

DANCE MINISTRY REHEARSAL SCHEDULE

DANCES OF PRAISE III

JUNE 13, 2004

MISSISSIPPI BLVD. CHRISTIAN CHURCH

4:00 p.m.

DATE/PLACE	TIME	SONG	DANCERS
Tues., April 20, 2004 4th Floor	5:30 p.m. 6:00 p.m. 6:30 p.m. 7:00 p.m. – 7:30 p.m.	Bible Study/Warm-up The Presence/Lord God's Favor Holy	Ensemble Ensemble Ensemble Small Group
Tues., April 27, 2004 4th Floor	5:30 p.m. 6:00 p.m. 6:30 p.m. 7:00 p.m. – 7:30 p.m.	Bible Study/Warm-up Glorious Hallelujah It's A New Season	Ensemble Ensemble Ensemble Duet
Sat., May 8, 2004 4th Floor	11:00 a.m. 11:30 a.m. 12:00 p.m. 12:30 p.m. 1:00 p.m. – 2:00 p.m. 2:00 p.m.-3:00 p.m.	Bible Study Warm-up Tap We Magnify/Name Let Us Worship You I Love Jesus/God Is Good	Ensemble Ensemble Small Group Ensemble Small Group/Guests Children Participating in Children's Sabbath May 30, 2004
Sat., May 15, 2004 4th Floor	11:00 a.m. 11:30 a.m. 12:00 p.m. 12:30 p.m. 1:00 p.m. 1:30 p.m. 2:00 p.m.-3:00 p.m.	Bible Study Warm-up Ark of The Covenant We Magnify/Name Tap Let Us Worship You I Love Jesus/God is Good	Ensemble Ensemble Small Group Ensemble Small Group Small Group/Guests Children Participating in Children's Sabbath May 30, 2004
Sat., May 22, 2004 4th Floor	11:00 a.m. 11:30 a.m. 12:00 p.m. 12:30 p.m. 1:00 p.m. 1:30 p.m. 2:00 p.m.-3:00 p.m.	Bible Study/Warm-up Ark of the Covenant Tap We Magnify/Name Glorious Hallelujah I Love Jesus/God is Good	Ensemble Small Group Small Group Ensemble Ensemble Ensemble Children Participating in Children's Sabbath May 30, 2004

Sat., May 29, 2004 4th Floor	11:00 a.m. 11:30 a.m. 12:00 p.m. 12:30 p.m. 1:00 p.m. 1:30 p.m. 2:00 p.m.-3:00 p.m.	Bible Study/Warm-up Collage/or Duet Holy Presence/Lord It's A New Season God's Favor I Love Jesus/God is Good	Ensemble Small Group Small Group Ensemble Duet Ensemble Children Participating in Children's Sabbath May 30, 2004
Sun., May 30, 2004 Sanctuary	10:00 a.m./One Service	Children's Sabbath	Children/Different Cultures
Sat., June 5, 2004 Sanctuary	11:00 a.m. – 2:00 p.m.	Run Through Both Acts	Ensemble
*Tues., June 8, 2004 Sanctuary	5:30 p.m. – 8:00 p.m.	Run Through Both Acts	Narrators Sound/Video Guest Ministries Guest Dancers Props
*Thurs., June 10, 2004 Sanctuary	5:30 p.m. – 8:00 p.m.	Run Through Both Acts	Narrators Sound/Video Guest Ministries Guest Dancers Props

*Sound/Video/Audio Staff Requested to be at Rehearsals

29

Pre—concert Set—up

Make sure all of the chairs are removed from choir stand and pulpit area

*** Projector in Baptismal with backdrop logo in it

*** Screen in the center of back choir row with white curtains and rainbow fringes set—up on both sides of screen

** Blue Throne is place in center of row directly under screen

** 24 folding chairs are placed around the throne on each side (maybe 4 chairs to a row going down diagonally

** Easel is set on the row of the left side of the curtains with the sign "*Praise Into His Presence*"

DANCE	DANCERS	COSTUMES	STAGE PROPS	BODY/HAND PROPS
"Holy"	Latoya/Shandra/Pat/Marica/ Denita/Jessica/Jocelyn/Krisden	*White Unitard/Skirt *Black Ballet Shoes **8 Angel Cloth Wings	***Fog Machine	**4 Beast Masks (lion/man/eagle/ox) **4 Angel Wing Headbands **4 Pairs Angel Wings Ankle Bands
Characters	God – Robert Roby or Pastor Thomas	**White Robe	**Blue Throne	**Mask
	24 Elders-Spiritual Officers	**White Robes	**24 Chairs	**24 Crowns

Stage Directions: Keep throne out there for the next dance, but remove the 24 chairs during the next narration.

Prop Directions: Props/Masks/Crowns/Wings are attached to dancers! Music starts first.

Audio: Music starts first after narration. (Cut 1, Disc 1)

Video:
1. Spotlight on narrator at sign language podium.
2. Medium range close—up on baptism while God, the angels and the elders enter from the choir stand.
3. After the dance begins move camera to the pulpit during the whole dance until the end.
4. Follow the dancers as they move down the two center aisles.

Screens:
1. Type Scene One, which is *Praise Into His Presence*.
2. Show narrator and put their name and the dance ("Holy"). The first narrator is Denita Hedgeman, Minister of Dance and Choreographer.
3. Keep focus in pulpit and choir stand until end of dance when the dancers run into the two center aisles.
4. In the middle of dance show at the narrators podium, Crystal Briggs.

DANCE	DANCERS	COSTUMES	STAGE PROPS	BODY/HAND PROPS
"Shouts of Joy"	Small Ensemble—**4 Priests**-Ron R./Maestro/Ron E./Ron H.	**White Robes **Ephods *Sandals	**Ark of The Covenant **Table for Ark (option)	
	4 Singers-Jessie/Gwen/Frances/ Sharonda	**White Robes or similar as scripture states 1 Chron. 15		***Tambourines/ Instruments
Character	David – Zurich Thomas or Robert R.	**Ephod **Short Robe ***Sandals		***Trumpet

*   Dancers' Personal Costumes/Items
** Church's Property
*** Personal/Burrowed Items

Stage Directions: The Ark will be brought in from the back of the church in the right center aisle by male dancers. Female dancers will carry in their own hand prop instruments. Dancers come in first before music.

Keep Ark up on platform during next song.

Audio:

1. Play Cut 2 during the trumpet sound.
2. Pause music while the dancers are marching in chanting carrying the ark down the right center aisle.
3. Take pause to (cut 3) off of music after dancers bow down to worship The Ark of the Covenant.

Video:

1. Show narrator at sign language table.
2. Follow dancers down right center aisle up to the pulpit area.
3. They will put the ark down in the choir stand and then come down to dance in the pulpit. (Medium range close—up)

Screens:

1. Show narrator and type in Allen Hammond.
2. Type in dance title, "Shouts of Joy".
3. Follow dancers down the right center aisle up to the pulpit.
4. They will put the ark down in the choir stand and then come down to dance in the pulpit.

DANCE	DANCERS	COSTUMES	STAGE PROPS	BODY/HAND PROPS
"Presence of The Lord Is Here"	Ensemble	*White Unitard/Skirt *Black Ballet Shoes **White Praise Robes	None	

Stage Directions: Dancers come out in positions before music starts. Take down Ark and throne and change easel sign to "*Worship*" after this song.

Audio:

1. No narration!
2. Dancers enter first, then put music on (Cut 4).

Video:

1. Show dancers on pulpit during their solo at the beginning.
2. When music gets faster and dancers enter in, show them coming in from all doors and choir stand.

Screen:

1. No narration!
2. Type in name of song, "The Presence of the Lord Is Here".
3. Show dancers and audience during this piece.

*   Dancers' Personal Costumes/Items
**   Church's Property
*** Personal/Burrowed Items

Screen:

1. No narration!
2. Type in name of song, "The Presence of the Lord Is Here."
3. Show dancers and audience during this piece.

DANCE	DANCERS	COSTUMES	STAGE PROPS	BODY/HAND PROPS
"Let Us Worship Him"	Small Ensemble	*TBA		
Participants	Flag Bearer-Robert Roby	Black	***Walker/**Chair	***Big Jesus Flag
	Handicapped-Angela Barksley	TBA		
	4 Deaf Ministry	TBA		
	4 Women	TBA		
	4 Small Children	TBA		
	4 Men	TBA		

Stage Directions: Flag Bearer comes out first with music. Angela is center stage sitting in chair with walker and Zurick is standing beside her.

Audio:
1. Narration first.
2. Music starts first. (Cut 5)

Video:
1. Close—up on narrator at sign language table.
2. Close—up on solo flag bearer coming in from side door on the band side. Follow him across the front of the communion table to the front of the organ to the up in the pulpit.
3. Medium range to center stage to focus on handicapped dancer and blind dancer for 2 & 3 verses.
4. Pan out a little to capture the deaf ministry on the pulpit and steps during 4th verse.
5. Focus behind them as two little girls dance in on each side of the pulpit to center then follow them up to the choir stand during 5th verse.
6. Men coming running in from the choir stand doors to center. Follow them out to the aisles and then back up to the pulpit.
7. Keep the camera on the pulpit wide range for the rest of the song.

Screens:
1. Show narrator and type in their name, Greg Turner.
2. Type in Scene 2–WORSHIP
3. Follow the video directions above.

* Dancers' Personal Costumes/Items
** Church's Property
*** Personal/Burrowed Items

DANCE	DANCERS	COSTUMES	STAGE PROPS	BODY/HAND PROPS
"It's A New Season"	Pat	*White Unitard *Black Ballet Shoes ***Gold Palazzo Pants/Top ***White Gloves/Makeup		***2 Streamers ***Big Flag ***Basket with money/video/alcohol bottle
	Denita	*White Unitard *Black Ballet Shoes ***Purple Palazzo Pants/Top ***White Gloves/Makeup		***2 Streamers ***Rainbow Streamer ***Basket with money/cigarettes/bag

Stage Directions: Have 2 Streamers/Rainbow Streamer/Big Flag/ and Baskets out on floor of the pulpit before dancers come out. Dancers come out with music.

Costume Assistants: After this dance, Pat and Denita will need someone to quickly help them change into their rainbow dresses before the next song. Have Denita's rainbow short streamer and rainbow long streamer. There will be no narration before the next song. Please be at the door waiting for them.

Audio: Music first (Cut 6)

Video:
1. Show Narrator at side podium.
2. Follow dancers in pulpit to the audience back into the pulpit at the beginning of the dance.
3. At the end, follow them out down the two center aisles.

Screens:
1. Show narrators and type their names, Crystal Briggs and Carol Wright.
2. Type Scene 3–*Your Time.*
3. Type in dancers names, Denita Hedgeman and Patricia Jones.
4. Follow video directions stated above.

*   Dancers' Personal Costumes/Items
** Church's Property
*** Personal/Burrowed Items

DANCE	DANCERS	COSTUMES	STAGE PROPS	BODY/HAND PROPS
"God's Favor"	Ensemble	*Rainbow Dresses *Black Ballet Shoes *White Gloves/Makeup		*Individual Rainbow Streamers
6 Soloists	Kierra/Maya/Tatika/Elizabeth/Jessica W./Marica	*Rainbow Dresses *Black Ballet Shoes **Colorful Gloves		*Individual Rainbow Streamers
Banner Runners	Pat/Gwen	Same	**Billow Banner	*Same
4 Basket Girls	Adjua/Jocelyn/Cherie/Kierra	Same		*Same with baskets
Flag Leader	Denita	Same		***Same with Long Rainbow Streamer

Stage Directions: Place Billow Banner inside sanctuary by the door on the band side. Dancers enter first.

Audio:

1. No narration! Dancers enter first (Cut 7)
2. Leo or musician will play reprise while the congregation dances afterwards.

Video:

1. 1st verse, show solo dancers on stage.
2. Chorus—show dancers in aisles.
3. Repeat directions like verse 1 and chorus.
4. Show two dancers running with the billow banner over the congregation (pew section left, center, then right)
5. Pan back and forth from the pulpit to the front and sides as the dancers are pulling people from the congregation to build the rainbow hand chain around the church.

DANCE	DANCERS	COSTUMES	STAGE PROPS	BODY/HAND PROPS
"Mercy Saw Me"	Betty Douglas	*Dress *Gold Robe	**Chair	
Characters	Two Men at the End (Bringing her Robe Out)	*Black Pants/T-Shirts *Black Shoes		

Stage Directions: Place chair out center stage before music starts. Change easel sign to *Testimony of God's Mercy*.

Dancers gives testimony first and then takes her position before the music starts.

Audio:

1. Dancer will narrate and testify at the podium.
2. Start music when she gets in place in pulpit in chair (Cut 8).

Video:

1. Close—up on dancer at podium.
2. Medium range of her dancing in pulpit (verse 1 and chorus).
3. Follow her as she ministers in the audience (verse 2).
4. Follow her to podium as she testifies again (chorus)
5. Follow her back up to the pulpit as she finishes the dance.

Screens:

1. Show dancer at the podium and type in her name, Betty Douglas and Scene 4–*Testimony Of God's Mercy.*
2. Same as the video directions above.

* Dancers' Personal Costumes/Items
** Church's Property
*** Personal/Burrowed Items

DANCE	DANCERS	COSTUMES	STAGE PROPS	BODY/HAND PROPS
"Glorious"	Ensemble	*Rainbow Dresses		**Flowers in Hair

Stage Directions: Change easel sign to *Your Purpose.* Music starts first. Reprise starts again for dancers and audience to come back in.

Audio:

1. Narration first.
2. Music starts first (Cut 9).
3. Let reprise pick back up.

Video:

1. Show narrator at side podium.
2. Show dancers coming in all doors.

3. When dancers start building the rhumba line, follow them out into all four aisles pulling people from the audience.
4. During the first part of the reprise, show the two dancers on stage doing the salsa.
5. When chorus starts back up, follow dancers and audience back in down the same aisles.

Screens:
1. Show narrator at side podium and type their name, Oscar Sueing.
2. Type in Scene 5–*Your Purpose*.

DANCE	DANCERS	COSTUMES	STAGE PROPS	BODY/HAND PROPS
"Hallelujah"	Ensemble	*Colorful African Attire (Pants)		
Flags	Elizabeth/Andreanna	Same		***2 Tambourines
	Amber or Melanie	Same		***Baton
	Jalicia/Christian/Marica/Deanna/Mea/Jada	Same		***6 Flags/Streamers

Stage Directions: Music starts first. Change easel sign to *He's Worthy* during narration.

Audio:
1. Narration first!
2. Music starts first (Cut 1, Disc 2)

Video:
1. Show narrator at side podium.
2. Show dancers coming in from all doors.
3. Keep wide range of pulpit and front until solos, then keep it in pulpit.

Screens:
1. Show narrator and type name, Marcia Matthews.
2. Type in Scene 6–*He's Worthy*.
3. Same as video directions above.

DANCE	DANCERS	COSTUMES	STAGE PROPS	BODY/HAND PROPS
"How Great Thou Art"	Adea Sessoms	**Colorful Dress from Past Easter Service (Leo's Office) *Pointe Shoes		

Audio:
1. No narration!
2. Music starts first (cut 2).

Video:
1. No narration!
2. Dancer starts coming from top row of choir stand to the pulpit.
3. Follow her down front of the communion table and out down the aisles.
4. She will finish back center stage.

Screens:
1. No narration!
2. Type in soloist, Adea Sessoms.
3. Same as video directions stated above.

* Dancers' Personal Costumes/Items
** Church's Property
*** Personal/Burrowed Items

DANCE	DANCERS	COSTUMES	STAGE PROPS	BODY/HAND PROPS
"He's Always On My Mind"	Cayla/Mary/Maya/Jessica B./Shandra/Ariel/Adero/Frances/Kierra/Jessica W.	*Black Pants **"Still Here" Sequin Tops or *White Unitard with *Purple Pants from new outfit *Tap Shoes	**Tap Board	

Stage Directions: Place Tap Board out before music starts. Change easel sign to *Love*. Dancers are in positions first.

Audio:
1. Narration first.
2. Dancers are in place first. (Cut 3)

Video:
1. Show narrator at side podium.
2. Keep video on medium range in the center of the pulpit.

Screens:
1. Show narrator at side podium.
2. Type in their name, Ron Hill.
3. Type in Scene 7–LOVE.
4. Keep screens on dancers taping center stage.

DANCE	DANCERS	COSTUMES	STAGE PROPS	BODY/HAND PROPS
"Dancing So Close To The Fire"	John/Denita	*Black Pants **Demon Tops	***Fog Machine ***Strobe Light	
Characters	2 Prayer Warriors – Business Person and a Clergyman Angel	*Suit/Clergy Collar **White Robe/Wings/Halo		*Briefcase ***Flash Paper Gun

Stage Directions: Change easel sign to *Spiritual Warfare*. Music starts first.

Audio:
1. Narration first.
2. Music starts first (Cut 4)

Video:
1. Show narrator at side podium.
2. Medium/Close—up in pulpit during whole song until near the end.
3. Medium range view in choir stand of prayer warriors and angel throwing fire on the demons.
4. Show center stage as demons are dying.

Screens:
1. Show narrator at side podium.
2. Type in narrator's name, Flo Roach.

3.   Type in Scene 8–*Spiritual Warfare*.

*Lights and strobe light need to flicker in the middle of song when dancers are rolling around uncontrollably.

DANCE	DANCERS/SINGERS	COSTUMES	STAGE PROPS	BODY/HAND PROPS
"Angels"	Flo Roach	Pastor's Robe		Mike

Audio:
1.   No narration!
2.   Start music first.

Video:
1.   Medium shot while demons are being dragged off stage.
2.   Close—up of singer while she is singing.

Screens:
1.   No narration!
2.   Soloist—Flo Roach

*   Dancers' Personal Costumes/Items
** Church's Property
*** Personal/Burrowed Items

DANCE	DANCERS	COSTUMES	STAGE PROPS	BODY/HAND PROPS
"We Magnify Your Name"	MBCC Dancer Ministry St. Andrew AME Church Abundant Grace Fellowship Nubian Dance Theater	*Purple Pants/Top Own Own Own		***Big Flag

Stage Directions: Change easel sign to *Victory Praise*. About 50 to 60 dancers are lined up outside of all doors. Music starts first.

Audio:
1.   Narration first!
2.   Music first (Cut 5)

Video:
1.   Show narrator at side podium.

2. During Music intro, show St. Andrew dancers running in all doors and keep wide range with sometimes close—ups (verse 1)

3. Show only pulpit and steps while next group, Abundant Grace is dancing (verse 2).

4. Show only pulpit and steps while next group, Nubian Dance Theater.

5. Show the cannon section of everybody and all four aisles.

6. Show pulpit and front area while MBCC Dance Ministry is dancing.

7. Zoom back out as the other ministries join us.

Screens:

1. Type narrator's name, Ben Greene.

2. Type in Scene 9–*Victory Praise*.

3. Type in groups names as their team is ministering. Group #1–St. Andrew AME. Church, "Ministers in Motions"—Director, Minister Sarita Guffin. Group #2–Abundant Grace Fellowship, "Ministry in Motion"—Director, Erica Anderson. Group #3–Nubian Dance Theater—Choreographer, John Sullivan. Group #4– MBCC Dance Ministry— Director, Minister Denita Hedgeman

*   Dancers' Personal Costumes/Items
**   Church's Property
*** Personal/Burrowed Items

30

Good Afternoon! I'm Dr. Denita Hedgeman, Minister of Dance and Choreographer for the MBCC Dance Ministry and I welcome you to "Dances of Praise III." This is our 3rd annual concert and each year God takes His message higher and higher through dance. This year we are going to minister through prophetic and congregational dance, praise and worship, Jewish, Latin, African Jazz, ballet, tap, warfare dance, flags, billow banners and hip-hop. We will also feature the physically and hearing impaired and several guest dance ministries from across the city.

This first piece, called Holy, is a prophetic dance. A prophetic dance is unchoreographed, spontaneous and given by the Holy Spirit. Psalms 100:4 says to enter into his gates with thanksgiving and into his courts with praise: be thankful unto Him and bless his name. This means that before the presence of the Lord can come down, we have to praise and thank Him whole heartily. This will usher Him in. During this dance, you will have the opportunity to praise, dance and worship as the Holy Spirit leads you. This scene will be a mini version of heaven including God, some angels and creatures of a man, lion, eagle and calf. The scriptures are from Isaiah 6:2–3, Rev. 4:8 and 5:11–12.

The Ark of The Covenant/
The Presence of The Lord Is Here

Narrator—Mr. Allen Hammond
Author—Dr. Denita Hedgeman

We will continue to usher in The Lord's presence in the next two pieces. We just had a glimpse of the end and what it will be like in heaven and now we are going to celebrate the earlier style of praise and worship. Most of the dances in the Bible were Jewish and done in a circle. One highlight was in 1 Chronicles 15 when David and the Levites carried the Ark of The Covenant to the city of David while shouting, dancing and playing instruments. The Ark of the Covenant was first mentioned in the Bible in Exodus 25 where Moses was instructed to build a Tabernacle (or tent) for the Israelites to worship God. Placed in the "Holy of Holies," The Ark was the most sacred object in the Tabernacle. It was made of arcadia wood and overlaid with gold. Atop the Ark were two gold cherubs that stood with their wings covering the area known as the "Mercy Seat." The Ark contained three items—two stone tablets bearing the inscription of the Ten Commandments, the rod of Aaron and the golden pot of Manna. The Ark was where God manifested His presence on earth and went ahead of the Israelites wherever they traveled. Let's go back in time and celebrate with the Israelites to the song "Shouts of Joy" and then come on into the present with "The Presence of The Lord Is Here!"

Let Us Worship Him
Narrator—Mr. Greg Turner
Author—Dr. Denita Hedgeman

John 4:23 says "But the hour cometh, and now is, when the true worshippers shall worship the Father in spirit and in truth: for the Father seeketh such to worship him." God seeks those who really worship him. It pleases God when we worship him with our whole hearts. It doesn't matter how we worship him. We can bow, cry, close our eyes, clap, sing, dance, lay prostrate before him, stomp our feet or however we want to express our love to him. We should be thankful that we could use our limbs or bodies anyway we please to worship him. (Insert Zerick's testimony) In this next piece, you will see some people who have limited use of their limbs or senses, but will be able to praise God in their own way. There will also be small children, women and men worshipping God to "Let Us Worship Him."

It's a New Season/God's Favor
Narrators—Mrs. Crystal Briggs, Mrs. Carol Wright
Author—Dr. Denita Hedgeman

How many of you believe it's your season? How many of you believe that right now you can reach up and grab all of the blessings God has for you such as power, love, peace, favor, prosperity, jobs, new relationships, healing and deliverance? Eccl. 3:1 says "To everything there is a season, and a time to every purpose under heaven." This is definitely the time to gain God's favor! Psalms 5:12 says "For thou, Lord, wilt bless the righteous: with favour wilt thou compass him as with a shield."

In the next two dances, you will have a chance to receive and participate. In the dance, "It's A New Season," receive the gifts of prosperity and celebrate with the dancers as they throw their strongholds in the fire so they can move into their new season. In the dance "God's Favor," some of you will be asked to hold hands and join in the rainbow line of agreement with the dancers to signify

God's favor and covering over the church and in your life. Also, take your hand, scarf, program or streamer and wave them along with the dancers to the movements—faithfulness, Alpha, Omega, Hallelujah, Reverse Hallelujah, Banner Over Me, and Glorious. Receive the dancers at this time.

Glorious
Narrator—Mr. Oscar Sueing
Author—Dr. Denita Hedgeman

Did you know that you were created to praise God and make his name Glorious? I Thess. 5:16–18 says to "Rejoice evermore. Pray without ceasing. In everything give thanks: for this is the will of God in Christ Jesus concerning you. This is his will!" It also says in Psalms 148:5 & 12–13, "Let them praise the name of the Lord: for he commanded, and they were created. Both young men and maidens; old men and children: Let them praise the name of the Lord: for his name alone is excellent; for his glory is above the earth and heaven." In this next piece, you will have the opportunity to celebrate what you were created to do. The dancers will pull some of you from the audience to participate in a Rhumba line to a Latin beat to "Glorious."

Hallelujah/How Great Thou Art
Narrator—Ms. Marcia Matthews
Author—Mrs. Carol Wright

Who can describe the greatness and awesomeness of God? Just think of all of His names. Jehovah Jireh, Jehovah Raphe, Jehovah Shalom, El Elyon, El Shaddai, Adonai, and we could go on, but to sum it up, he said, "I AM!!!!" Just His names tell how great He is! Think about it, God said "Let there be . . . and there is!" God reminds us Himself how great He is when He answered Job in Job chapters 38–41. Just read it for yourself! And because He is so great, All we can do is give Him the highest Praise, Hallelujah! For He is worthy to be praised!

In these next two pieces, the highest praise will be lifted with colorful flags, streamers, instruments, and praise dancing. *Hallelujah, You're Worthy To Be Praised!*

And the awesomeness of God will continue to flow through classical ballet and Pointe as Adea Sessoms tells the Lord through dance. *How Great Thou Art!*

Always On My Mind
Narrator—Mr. Ron Hill
Author—Mrs. Carol Wright

How many of you have ever been in love?
How does it feel? How do you act?
You can't wait to call that person and
you're on the phone for hours.
When you are with them, you can't get close enough.
You want to be in their presence.

They are always on your mind!

God created us to worship Him, to be in fellowship with Him,
to Love Him.
Matthew 22:37 tells us "You should love the Lord thy God with all
your heart, with all your soul and with all your mind."

Psalms 26:2 says, "Test me O Lord, and try me, examine my heart
and mind for your love is ever before me . . ."

There are always benefits to loving God and keeping Him on your
mind, because that is just how and who He is!!!!

One benefit in Psalms 25:15 says, "My eyes are ever on the Lord, for
only He will release my feet from the snare."

How fitting, that in this next piece (beginner tappers) will allow
the Lord to release their feet from the snare and illustrate that if

we love Him, if He is always on our mind. No matter what the circumstance, he will keep you in perfect peace.

You can be like these dancers and tap your way on through that problem because the great I AM has it all in control.

Always On My Mind

Dancing So Close to the Fire
Narrator—Ms. Flo Roach
Author—Mrs. Carol Wright

Proverbs 16:16 says, "Pride goes before destruction, a haughty spirit before a fall."

Ephesians 6:12 says, "For we wrestle not against flesh and blood but against principalities, against powers, against the rulers of the darkness of this world, against spiritual wickedness in high places."

Then we must put on the whole armour of God so that we will be able to stand. We must be ready! Satan's kingdom is organized. He comes to kill, steal and destroy and he has a plan.

We have a plan too. The Word of God is our plan. We are to be ready with our armour on. James 4:7 says, "Submit yourselves therefore to God. Resist the devil and he will flee from you."

Your title, your economic status, your pride, and your ego can't do anything for you in your fight against the devil. But your submission to God, you putting on the full armour of God listed in Ephesians 6, and the angels hearkening unto the voice of His word will keep you from the destruction of the fire.

This action packed dance theatre dramatization will illustrate the spirit of pride and the spirit of haughtiness that seeks to destroy us in our lives. It doesn't matter who you are—preacher, teacher, or whoever, these spirits are out to cause you destruction. This dance shows us that even these spirits are in discord with one another, and that submission to God and the power of prayer is so strong, that it will cause the evil spirits' destruction.

Dancing So Close To The Fire!

We Magnify your Name!
Narrator—Mr. Ben Greene
Author—Dr. Denita Hedgeman

God's name has truly been lifted up in praise and dance in this concert in every way possible. We've witnessed solos, congregational, worship, prophetic, colors, different cultures, biblical history, testimonies, dance theater, and the different forms of Christian dance illustrated by children, youth, men and women. Now it's time to celebrate God's goodness with other dance ministries. In this finale, you will experience the different styles from St. Andrew A.M.E. Church called Ministry in Motion under the direction of Minister Sarita Guffin; Abundant Grace Fellowship called Ministers in Motion under the direction of Erica Anderson; the Nubian Dance Theatre under the direction of John Sullivan; and our own MBCC Dance Ministry under the direction of Minister Dr. Denita Hedgeman. They will minister to "We Magnify Your Name."

31

Dr. Denita Hedgeman has the ultimate joy in answering her call to preach, teach, minister, prophesy, evangelize and testify on how good God is, and win souls for Jesus Christ through the arts. She is one of the Mid-South's most dynamic artists as a choreographer, singer, dancer, actress, instructor, facilitator, motivational speaker, adjudicator and author. She has been dancing since the age of six and has been a professional choreographer since the age of 14.

Dr. Hedgeman has performed and choreographed for many church presentations, concerts, movies, TV series, MTV videos, off-Broadway and community plays, commercials, training films, background vocals for local and national recording artists and other special events. Some of her credits include "*Great Balls of Fire,*" "*Take Me Back To Beale,*" "*Elvis Presley Rockin' Tonight,*" "*The Trials of Rosie O'Neal,*" S*chilling, Cablevision* and *Alfred's* commercials; *Jason D. Williams, Hal Ketchum and The Book's music videos; background singing work for Eric Johnson and the rock group Foreigner; Federal Express Industrial film;* off-Broadway play, "*Mama Don't*"; *A*BC *and WMC-TV Easter Specials* and *Umoja Kamaru* for Mississippi Blvd. Christian Church; *Overton High School Show Choir, Trezevant High and Snowden Middle School's choreographer,* theatrical productions such as "*Taking It To The Streets*", *"Journey Into Paradise", "Luscious Lived",*

"Listen Children", "Harambee", "A Matter of Life and Death", "Where Did We Go Wrong", and a pre-show for the *Sunset Symphony* featuring Isaac Hayes.

Other credits include an interview and performance on Trinity Broadcasting Network (TBN), PM Magazine, at The Bobby Jones International Gospel Music Industry Retreat in Las Vegas and Cable Channel 17 show, "Holistically You"; a featured solo dancer with Howard Hewitt during his concert at the Cannon Center for the Performing Arts to his gospel song, "Joy"; an opening dance solo performance for the Breath of Life Christian Center's 20th Anniversary at the Orpheum Theatre which featured Helen Baylor, Out of Eden, Nicholas and Jonathan Slocumb; a solo dance for Kenneth Davis' Debut CD Concert; dance performance for The School of Prophets' graduation; a dancer for WDIA's 50th Anniversary; one of the opening dancers for Christian Recording Artist, Tonex; a dancer and guest speaker for the Women on the Frontline for Jesus' Conference; and choreographer for pageants, reunions, weddings, bridal shows, graduations, society groups and for one of the Southern Heritage Classic Fashion Shows. Also, she is an adjudicator for talent competitions, a motivational speaker, a liturgical dance and career development workshop facilitator and has assisted churches in starting or working with their dance ministries such as Golden Leaf M.B. Church, Spirit of Life Healing Wings, St. Luke M.B. Church, Castalia Baptist Church, the youth of World Overcomers Church, Greater Community Temple, Unity Christian Center, The Liturgical Dance Institute at Shiloh Baptist Church in Olive Branch, MS and Inward Faith Outreach Ministries in Topeka, KS.

Dr. Hedgeman has ministered, performed and choreographed in France, The Bahamas, Hawaii, Jamaica, Canada, New York, California, Atlanta, Chicago, Florida, Houston, Pittsburgh, Indianapolis, Topeka, Washington, D.C., Oklahoma, Las Vegas, Ohio, Mississippi and Memphis. She has also won an award for "Best Choreography" in Nice, France.

Dr. Hedgeman earned a Bachelor of Communication and Fine Arts degree in Journalism with a concentration in Advertising from

The University of Memphis (formerly known as Memphis State). She has also received a Master of Religious Fine Arts in Dance and a Doctor of Ministry in Religious Dance from Friends International Christian University (FICU) in Merced, California. She has her certification in prophetic ministry and prophetic counseling and is an ordained and licensed minister through The School of Prophets, a division of Ray Self Ministries, Inc. in Olive Branch, MS. She has been appointed by Christian Dance Fellowship (CDF) to be the Dance Ministry State Coordinator for Tennessee. She is a member of the National Liturgical Dance Network (NLDN), the International and National Christian Dance Fellowship (ICDF)/(CDF) and Society for Human Resource Management (SHRM). She is also the Founder and Choreographer of the group Disciples of Dance. She is the author of "The Guidelines to Starting and Maintaining a Dance Ministry in the Church." She has been the Minister of Dance/Choreographer of the Dance Ministry at Mississippi Blvd. Christian Church since 1990 and is currently the Director of Career Services at LeMoyne-Owen College in Memphis, Tennessee.

Program

Praise Into His Presence

Holy . . . . Judith Christie McAllister

Shouts of Joy. . . . . Messianic Praise

The Presence Of the Lord Is Here . . . . Byron Cage

Worship

Let Us Worship Him . . . . Yolanda Adams

Your Time

It's A New Season. . . . . Israel & New Breed

God's Favor. . . . . Donald Lawrence

Testimony of God's Mercy

Mercy Saw Me . . . . T.D. Jakes Best Selections

*Solo—Betty Douglas

Your Purpose

Glorious . . . . Martha Munizzi

Intermission (10 Minutes)

He's Worthy

Hallelujah: You're Worthy. . . . . Judith Christie McAllister

How Great Thou Art . . . . Sandi Patti

*Solo—Adea Sessoms

Love

He's Always On My Mind . . . . Phoebe Hines

Spiritual Warfare

We Dance To Close To The Fire . . . . Tommy Faragher

*Duet—Dr. Denita Hedgeman & John Sullivan

Angels. . . . . Richard Smallwood

*Soloist—Flo Roach

Victory Praise

We Magnify Your Name...................... Shekinah Glory

**Finale with Guest Dance Ministries

Shabach .... Bryon Cage

Curtain Call

Invitation To Discipleship.................Pastor Frank A. Thomas

*Student Choreography Project

**Guest Dance Ministries choreographed their featured section (combined sections choreographed by Dr. Denita Hedgeman)

2004 MBCC Dance Ministry

Dancers

Cayla Anderson
Cherie Anthony
Shandra Brock+
Jessica Brown
Jocelyn Brown
Maya Brown
Amber Buggs
Mea Byrd
*LaToya Chavers
*Ayana Clinton+
*Christian Dixon
Carmen Flowers
Shaquan Hampton
Adero Hardy
Adjua Hardy
Gwen Harvey
*Denita Hedgeman+
Alandra Jones
Kelsey Jones
*Patricia Jones+
Tatika Jones
Kierra Kimbrough
Mary Lindsey+
Sierra Martin
*Angela McCrackin
Jada McNeil
*Ariel Milton
Frances Moore+
Deanna Palmer

*Jalicia Russell
*Elizabeth Sueing
Andreanna Williams
*Krisden Williams+
Jessica Winters
Marica Wright

Guest Dancers

Angela Barksley
Maestro Byars
Betty Douglas
Ron Evans
Hannah Gray
Sharonda Hardy
Ron Hill
Alaina Perry
Ron Robinson
Adea Sessoms
John Sullivan
Jessie Towns

Guest Dance Ministries/Groups

Abundant Grace Fellowship, Ministers in Motion, Erica Anderson, Ministry Head/Choreographer

Nubian Dance Company, John Sullivan, Choreographer

St. Andrew AME Church, Ministry in Motion, Sarita Guffin, Minster of Dance/Choreographer

Cloverknook Center for the Blind, Robin Warren

MBCC Deaf Ministry, Ministry Leader-Sherrie Terrell, (Dancers) Carolyn Clay/Barbara Harrison/Kenyada Harrison (Interpreters) LaVerne Bobo, LaJuana Beasley and Tursha Hamilton

*Dance Captains
+ Bible Study Assistants

Acknowledgements

Stage Directors
Lethelea Jackson
Kerry Watkins

Narrators
Crystal Briggs
Ben Greene
Allen Hammond
Ron Hill
Marcia Matthews
Flo Roach
Oscar Sueing
Greg Turner

Program Design/ Invitations/flyers
Denita Hedgeman
Matthew Taylor, III

Stage/Propassistants
Daniel Brown
Shirley Calhoun-Wallace
Ron Hill
Jermaine Jones
Patrick Jones
Stephanie Jones
Leon Lee
Charles McNeill
Marcus Tate
Greg Turner

Staging
Grand Rental

Prop Design
Charles McNeill
Marvin Wright

Ministry Head
Leo Davis

Ministry Assistant
Carol Wright

Fundraising
Denita Hedgeman
Carol Wright
Lisa Yates

Prayer Covering
Mildred Nelson

Communications
Natalie Robinson

Elders
Margaret Beasley
Cheryl Bingham
LaVerne Bobo
Ricky Bobo

Marvin Wright
Jeff Young
Essie Clay

Costume Committee/Parent Assistants
Deborah Anthony
Tonya Brown
Lois Dixon
Betty Douglas
Sharonda Hardy
Linda Sueing
Mary Taylor
Amelia Williams
Valencia Watson
Carol Wright

MBCC Multi-media
Edith Kelly-Green, Media Manager
Ray Griffin, Media Coordinator
Calvin Miller, Video Coordinator
Tony Mitchell, Lighting
Darryl Evans, Audio Recording/Music Production

Clarence Boone
Patrick Briggs
Lonnie Coleman
Frederick Curry
Deborah DeWitt
Ben Greene
Ellen Gunn
Tessera Hardaway
Kenneth Hughes
Emily Jackson
Debbie Jones
Roscoe Jordan
Joseph Kyles
Joseph Lyles
Joyce Mathis
Cheryl Pettigrew
Julian Pettigrew
Elderidge Williams
Shadyne Williams

32

DANCE MINISTRY PERMISSION FORM

Name: _____ Date of Birth: _____

Address: _____ Phone # _____

Any Known Illness (es): _____

_____

Medication(s): _____

_____

Allergic to the Following: _____

_____

Emergency Contact: _____

Relation: _____

Phone #: _____ Alternate Phone #: _____

Insurance Carrier: _____ Insurance ID#: _____

Physician(s): _____

_____

The undersigned, a parent or legal guardian of _____

_____, agrees to hereby release, and forever
discharge the church, the leader, chaperones and volunteers from all
actions, claims, costs, expenses or damages of any kind growing out
of or related to any activity in which the undersigned or a member
of the immediate family of the undersigned participates during the
Dance Ministry Retreat/Sleepover and Field Trip to Casey Jones in
Jackson, TN, on June 15–16, 2001, during the hours 7:00 p.m. (Fri-

day) to 6:oo p.m. (Saturday). The participant is responsible for all costs regarding meals, shopping or extra activities during the trip. The undersigned, a parent or legal guardian of the immediate family of the undersigned, further acknowledges that this is a full and complete release for all injuries and damages which the participant during this retreat and trip may incur.

Signature: _____

Date: _____

Student's Signature: _____

33

Friday, June 15, 2001–7:00 *p.m.*

Welcome

Introduction of Participants

Praise Reports/Prayer Requests

Prayer

Bible Study/Book Review

Meditation Time/Song

Introduction of Speaker

Speaker–Della Perkins/Director, Christ The Rock Dance Ministry

Master Class–Della Perkins

Food

Presentations

View Video Tapes

Holy Ghost Party Dance

Games/Fellowship

Sleepover

Saturday, June 16, 2001

7:00 a.m.–Prayer of Thanksgiving

7:15 a.m.–Shower/Dress

8:15 a.m.–Light Continental Breakfast

9:00 a.m.–Clean Up Family Life Center

9:30 a.m.–Leave for Casey Jones Village

3:30 p.m.–Leave for Memphis

4:30 p.m.–Return to Memphis

34

Prayer

General Conference Information

Registration and Hotel Information

Conference and Roommate Sign-Up

Car Wash Information and Shift Sign-Up–Lisa Yates

Sponsorship Surprise

Testimony of Previous Conference from Dance Ministry Member–Jocelyn Brown

Review Video Excerpts from Last Year's Conference

35

DANCE CONFERENCE SIGN—UP SHEET

Name	Chaperone	Participant	Registered	Adult 10 & Under 18 & Under

36

August 24, 2003

Mr. Eddie Jones
Director of Operations
School Trans
1725 East Holmes Road
Memphis, TN 38116

Dear Mr. Jones:

Per your conversation with Mrs. Lisa Yates, I am writing regarding to request a sponsorship from your company for the Mississippi Blvd. Christian Church Dance Ministry to attend the Creative Arts Worship and Prophetic Conference in Rogers, AR. We need assistance to purchase bus transportation from Southern Stages, Inc.

We have approximately 40 people attending this conference ranging from 8 years old to adults. Some of them really want to go but can't afford the whole conference. They are going to have to pay for registration, hotel, spending money and bus transportation. Rogers, Arkansas is a six to seven hour drive, so this option would be the most practical mode of transportation.

This dance ministry is nationally known for its performances on Trinity Broadcast Network (TBN) and on The Bobby Jones Show in Las Vegas, Nevada. They specialize in ballet, jazz, tap, African, Latin, hip-hop, liturgical, drama, pantomime and spoken word.

Also, they minister across the city at special events, weddings, and churches and have an annual concert every June.

Attached is a proposal of sponsorship and a quote from Southern Stages, Inc. for your perusal. Feel free to contact me at (901) 942–7360 (w) or (901) 542–0032 (h) if you have any questions, suggestions or would like to discuss the proposed information further.

Thank you in advance for your consideration and support.

Sincerely,

Denita Hedgeman

Denita Hedgeman
Minister of Dance/Choreographer
Mississippi Blvd. Christian Church Dance Ministry

Proposal

Sponsorship Includes:

Bus Transportation to Rogers, AR $1950.00
October 10–13, 2003

Please make check payable to (Bus Company)!

37

September 17, 2003

Dr. Dellwyn Turnipseed-Bailey
30 E. Chickasaw Cove
Memphis, TN 38111

Dear Dr. Turnipseed-Bailey:

Thank you so much for your donation of $500.00 for bus transportation to Rogers, AR for the MBCC Dance Ministry Trip in October 2003. We greatly appreciate you making this conference a reality for the ministry. We could not have been able to afford the cost of the bus without your assistance.

This act of kindness and support will boost the ministry into a higher level of knowledge and creativity, now that they will have the opportunity to learn and fellowship with other praise dancers from all over the world at The Creative Arts Worship & Prophetic Conference.

We will never forget this gracious gesture from your heart. May God continue to bless you and your family.

Sincerely,

Denita Hedgeman

Denita Hedgeman
Minister of Dance/Choreographer
Mississippi Blvd. Christian Church Dance Ministry

38

To: Memphis City Schools/Shelby County Schools/Private School System

From: Denita Hedgeman
Director, Mississippi Boulevard Christian Church Dance Ministry

Date: September 8, 2003

Re: Creative Arts Worship & Prophetic Conference
Rogers, AR

Dear Principal/Teacher:

Please excuse the following student on the date(s) stated below to attend a Creative Arts Worship & Prophetic Conference in Rogers, AR, from October 10–13, 2003. The dance ministry from Mississippi Boulevard Christian Church will be participating in this conference.

This conference is a required event for the dancers to reflect on and learn more of the many facets of ministry through the arts as they develop personally, physically and spiritually. There will be ministries from all over the world participating in this conference. The students will learn dance, song, mime, puppets, acting, flags, banners, hip hop, African, streamers, Israeli dance, sign language, storytelling, liturgical, processionals, etc.

Most of the students will be on Fall break that weekend while others will need to be dismissed either by 12:00 p.m. on Friday, October 10, or on Monday, October 13 (date of travel return).

Each student's situation is different depending on the school system they attend. Attached is a copy of the conference schedule for your perusal. Thank you so much for your cooperation and support of this ministry.

_____   _____
Student's Name (Please Print)   Student's Signature

Please check the one that applies to the student

{ } Friday, October 10, 2003/Monday, October 13, 2003 (bus transportation and Shelby County Schools)

{ } Friday, October 10, 2003 (Memphis City Schools)

{ } Friday, October 10, 2003 (excused 12:00 p.m. for private schools)

_____   _____
Parent's Signature   Date

_____   _____
Principal's Signature   Date

_____   _____
Teacher's Signature   Date

To: College Professors
From: Denita Hedgeman
         Director, Mississippi Boulevard Christian
         Church Dance Ministry
Date: September 8, 2003
Re: Creative Arts Worship & Prophetic Conference
         Rogers, AR

Dear Principal/Teacher:

Please excuse the following student on the date(s) stated below to attend a Creative Arts Worship & Prophetic Conference in Rogers, AR from October 10–13, 2003. The dance ministry from Mississippi Boulevard Christian Church will be participating in this conference.

This conference is a required event for the dancers to reflect on and learn more of the many facets of ministry through the arts as they develop personally, physically and spiritually. There will be ministries from all over the world participating in this conference. The students will learn dance, song, mime, puppets, acting, flags, banners, hip hop, African, streamers, Israeli dance, sign language, storytelling, liturgical, processionals, etc.

Most of the students will be on Fall break that weekend while others will need to be dismissed for the entire trip.

Attached is a copy of the conference schedule for your perusal. Thank you so much for your cooperation and support of this ministry.

_____   _____
Student's Name (Please Print)   Student's Signature

Please check below

{ } Friday, October 10, 2003/Monday, October 13, 2003
    (bus transportation)

_____   _____
Parent's Signature   Date

_____   _____
Professor's Signature   Date

39

CREATIVE ARTS WORSHIP & PROPHETIC CONFERENCE

JOY SHOPPE

ROGERS, AR

EMBASSY SUITES HOTEL

MBCC DANCE MINISTRY

OCTOBER 10–13, 2003

BUS
Denita Hedgeman
Daniel Brown
Jessica Brown
Jocelyn Dyson Brown
Maya Brown
LaToya Chavers
Erin Collins
Sydney Collins
Angelica Deener
Christian Dixon
Betty Douglas
Tamarcus Douglas
**Kenneth Farmer
Kenthia Farmer
Carl Flake
Rachel Hawkins
Kierra Kimbrough
Mary Lindsey
Deborah Logan

*VAN
Tonya Brown
**Jada Flake
Carmen Flowers
**Joan T. Glenn
Alandra Jones
Patricia Jones
Patrick Jones
Jada Meeks

+CAR
Ameila Williams
Linda Sueing

Sierra Martin
Carol Mazique
**Angela McCracken
Bobbie Palmer
Deanna Palmer
Jason Powell
Jalicia Russell
Amena Smith
Larry Smith
Elizabeth Sueing
Lura Wade
Andreanna Williams
Krisden Williams
Carol Wright
Marica Wright
Lisa Yates

*CAR	*CAR
Dr. Dellwyn Turnipseed	Orlando Ross
Bria Bailey	Friend

+ Arrive Late
*Arrive Late/Leave Early
**Ride Bus Friday/Church Van Sunday

40

HOTEL ROOM ASSIGNMENTS

The Embassy Suites at Pinnacle
3303 Pinnacle Hills Parkway
Rogers, AR 72758 (Fayetteville, AR)
(479) 254–8400/1–800-EMBASSY
www.embassysuites.com

1. Denita Hedgeman-A
2. Mary Lindsay-A
3. Bobbie Palmer-A
4. LaToya Chavers-A
5. **Angela McCracken-A
6. Deanna Palmer-C

1. Lisa Yates-A
2. Carol Mazique-A
3. Rachel Hawkins-A
4. Jalicia Russell-C
5. Christian Dixon-C
6. Kenthia Farmer-C

1.*Tonya Brown-A
2.*Jada Meeks-A
3.*Patricia Jones-A
4.*Alandra Jones-C
5.*Carmen Flowers-C
6.Erin Collins-C

1. Deborah Logan-A
2. Carol Wright-A
3. Kierra Kimbrough-C
4. Marica Wright-C
5. Krisden Williams-C
6. Sydney Collins-C

1. Joycelyn Dyson Brown-A
2. Betty Douglas-A
3. Dr. Dellwyn Trunipseed-A
4. Jessica Brown-C
5. Maya Brown-C
6. Bria Bailey-C

1. Lura Wade-A
2.
3. **Joan Taylor-A
4. Sierra Martin-C
5. Angelica Deener-C
6. **Jada Flake-C

1. Carl Flake-A
2. Larry Smith-A
3. **Kenneth Farmer-A
4. *Patrick Jones-C
5. Jason Powell-C
6. Daniel Brown-C
7. Tamarcus Douglas-C

1. Amelia Williams-A
2. Linda Sueing-A
3. Andreanna Williams-C
4. Elizabeth Sueing
5. Erin Collins-C (Sunday night only)
6. Amena Smith-C

Double Tree Hotel
1. *Orlando Ross-A
2. *Friend-A

Super 8 Motel
1. Bus Driver

A=Adult
C=Child
*Arrive Late/Leave Early
**Leave Early

41

Mississippi Blvd. Christian Church
Dance Ministry
Embassy Suites
3303 Pinnacle Hills Parkway
Rogers, AR 72758
October 10–13, 2003

Directions to Church from Southern Stages, Inc.
Take I-40 West

Pass Little Rock Exit

Exit off on Madison Avenue

Turn left on Madison

Pass Bellevue (1st street) which is the street that the front of the church is facing

Turn left at next street which is Montgomery (back of church)

Pass two parking lots on the left and turn left into the 3rd parking lot (the building will say Family Life Center)

Travel Itinerary—Friday, October 10, 2003

5:20 a.m.	Arrive at church
5:30 a.m.	Load bus with luggage
6:00 a.m. ·	Leave church parking lot for trip
9:00 a.m.	Stop for a bathroom break
12:00 noon	Arrive tentatively in Rogers, AR
12:00 noon	Check-in bus driver at Super 8 (exit 85)
12:30 p.m.	Arrive at Embassy Suites (exit 83)
12:30 p.m.	Check-in, register for workshops, unpack
3:00 p.m.	Meet in lobby and have bus driver to take us to eat at exit 85 (strip of restaurants)
5:00 p.m.	Arrive back at Embassy Suites

Travel Itinerary—Monday, October 13, 2003

6:30 a.m.	Load luggage on bus
7:00 a.m.	Eat breakfast at hotel
8:00 a.m.	Leave for Memphis
11:00 a.m.	Stop for bathroom break
2:30 a.m.	Arrive in Memphis, tentatively

Bibliography

Anderson, Ken. (1996). *Where To Find It in The Bible–The Ultimate A to Z Resource.* Nashville: Thomas Nelson, Inc.

Boschman, Lamar. (1994). *A Heart of Worship.* Lake Mary: Charisma House.

Brown, Jocelyn. (2005). Prayer Request/Praise Report Form for Mississippi

Blvd. Christian Church Dance Ministry. Memphis: Unpublished raw data.

Butler, Stephanie. (2002). *My Body Is The Temple: Encounters and Revelations of Sacred Dance and Artistry.* Fairfax: Xulon Press.

Chagrin Valley Web Directory. (2001–2005). Chagrin Falls: Moriah Ministries. WebDezignCom.

Dutts, Lorelei. (2005). Celebrate Black History Month-Teach Students about African-American Contributions to Dance. *Dance Teacher.* Vol. 27, Number 2. New York: Lifestyle Media, Inc., 54–55.

Garies, Alison. (1998). *Warriors of Praise: An Instructional Notebook about Dancing Before The Lord.* Orange: West Coast Pageantry.

Hedgeman, Denita. (2005). Telephone Surveys to Various Denominations on Their Belief of Dance in the Church. Memphis: Unpublished raw data.

Hedgeman, Denita. (1990–2004). Workshop Handouts, Forms, Bible Study, Narrations/Choreography for Dances of Praise III Concert, etc. Memphis: Unpublished raw data.

Holy Bible–King James Version. (1982) Nashville: Holman Bible Publishers.

Jewish Customs and Traditions. (2005). Members.aol.com./santarpiap/jewish.html.

Kovacs, Ph.D., Aimee. (1996). *Dancing into the Anointing.* Shippensburg: Treasure House, An Imprint of Destiny Image Publishers, Inc.

Mears, Henrietta C. (1997). *What The Bible Is All About: Bible Handbook.* King James Bible Edition. Ventura: Regal Books from Gospel Light.

Morris, William, Editor. (1980). *The American Heritage Dictionary of the English Language.* Boston: Houghton Mifflin Company.

Nelson, Thomas. (1997, 1999). *The New Strong's Concise Concordance and Vine's Concise Dictionary of the Bible.* Two Bible Reference. Classics in One Handy Volume. Nashville: Thomas Nelson, Inc.

Rutherford, Pamela. *Make His Praise Glorious Manual.* Plano: Unpublished manuscript.

Stevenson, Ann. (2000, 2001). *Restoring the Dance: Seeking God's Order.* Shippenburg: Treasure House, An Imprint of Destiny Image Publishers, Inc.

Strong, James, LL.D., S.T.D. (2001). *The Strongest Strong's Exhaustive Concordance of the Bible.* 21st Century Edition. Grand Rapids: Zondervan.

Williams, Andrenna. (2004). Bible Study Discussion Handout. Memphis: Mississippi Blvd. Christian Church Dance Ministry. Unpublished raw data.

Wright, Carol. (2004). Narrations for Dances of Praise III Concert–Hallelujah, You're Worthy To Be Praised, How Great Thou Art, Always On My Mind. Memphis: Mississippi Blvd. Christian Church Dance Ministry. Unpublished raw data.

Wales, Jimmy, Sanger, Larry. (2001). Wikipedia, the Free Encyclopedia.

Zamar Patterns of Praise. (2000, 2001).Cleburne: Eastern Heights Church.

Praise for "Church Dance Ministry"

Have you had the desire to participate in or start a Liturgical Dance Ministry? Dr. Denita Hedgeman, has successfully compiled her doctoral research, testing, and application of dance ministry knowledge in this helpful publication.

As Founder and President of Friends International Christian University (FICU), I applaud, and have fully approved Denita's decision to publish this doctoral dissertation. I am pleased to recommend this book, as an exhaustive leadership manual, that will prove to edify and empower the Body of Christ. I am confident this book will serve as a powerful tool for anyone committed to the true ministry of dance.

When Dr. Denita Hedgeman graduated from FICU in 2005, the Lord sent prophetic words through my daughter Dr. Melinda Thomas, to Denita, declaring that her doctoral dissertation would one day be published. I am rejoicing now, as those prophetic words have been fulfilled, through the publication of this outstanding book!

I am truly honored to have the privilege of recommending this book to you.

E. N. Michaelson Ph.D.
Founder and President
Friends International Christian University